CHANGES

THE BUSY PROFESSIONAL'S GUIDE TO REDUCING STRESS, ACCOMPLISHING GOALS AND MASTERING ADAPTABILITY

MICHAEL DIETTRICH-CHASTAIN

CHANGES. The Busy Professional's Guide to Reducing Stress, Accomplishing Goals, and Mastering Adaptability.

ISBN-13: 978-1-7339397-0-6
Library of Congress Control Number: 2019904676

Are you interested in bulk copies for your group, organization or event? We offer bulk purchase discounts. Contact us to learn more: 828-365-6228

PRAISE FOR "CHANGES"

In *"Changes,"* Michael Diettrich-Chastain provides both a concise and compelling *"playbook"* for managing change in both our personal and professional lives. He examines the internal and external factors that impact our ability to successfully change and transform, and invites us to explore change from a spiritual and long-term perspective. I highly recommend this book for anyone charged with leading change in an organizational setting, or managing transitions in your personal life. Michael will challenge you to think differently and holistically, while providing the resources necessary to help you effectively manage change.

—WILLIAM L. SPARKS, PH.D. *Dennis Thompson Chair & Professor, Leadership McColl School of Business, Queens University of Charlotte*

As we grow, we calcify habits and patterns, and one of the best and hardest things we can do in our life is take control of our habits by examining them, breaking them, and then sticking to a new and better habit. Diettrich-Chastain makes that process clear and actionable, to allow both organizations and individuals to identify, action on and stick to change. A highly recommended resource that will open your eyes to the things that have been stuck in your life, and gives you a road map to finally shift them.

—ARIEL GARTEN, *Founder and CEO of Interaxon*

The quality of the questions we ask ourselves determines the quality of our lives! In CHANGES: The Busy Professional's Guide to Reducing Stress, Accomplishing Goals, and Mastering Adaptability, Michael Diettrich-Chastain masterfully guides us to three simple, brilliant questions that have the power to direct us to reduce stress, ignite momentum, and constantly keep us on track as change-thrivers! Michael teaches us how to use these questions as a GPS to great fulfillment, flexibility, and peace of mind both professionally and personally!

—BRIAN BIRO, *America's Breakthrough Coach, Author of Beyond Success and There are no Overachievers*

The more things stay the same, the more they don't! Everything is in a constant state of change...including YOU. Which is what makes this book so valuable. Drawing on his deep coaching and consulting experience, Michael Diettrich-Chastain provides insights, tools, and tips that are eminently effective and transformational.

—BILL TREASURER, *bestselling author of Courage Goes to Work.*

Michael has written the book every professional needs for today's constantly shifting marketplace. Changes - The Business Professional's Guide To Reduce Stress, Accomplish Goals and Master Adaptability is the ultimate guide to successfully navigating today's marketplace. Michael's book is powerful, packed with a deep understanding of how change impacts you, your business and your team. Which is enough reason to read this book - but then he takes it one step further. He loads this book with strategies and tools of exactly how to, what to and when to do it. I love this book - it is not a one-time read. This is the type of book you read, you reread and then you keep on your desk as your guide to mastering change.

—MERIDITH ELLIOT POWELL, *Business Growth Expert & Keynote Speaker*

Michael Diettrich-Chastain's debut book Changes is a comprehensive guide to creating your best life. Everyone wants to experience positive change. Humans are hardwired to evolve. Effectively executing that change, however, requires self-awareness and strategy - two things we aren't born with when we enter this world. Michael's book will provide you with a whole tool box of exercises and concepts to help you get from point A to point B, while enjoying the process.

—ALISON SHER, *author of The Millennial's Guide to Changing the World*

Michael Diettrich-Chastain's thorough and thoughtful book is a paean to the power—the imperative—of self-reflection in the work of creating positive change, both professionally and personally. He lucidly deconstructs the process of self-inquiry into its component parts, making it tangible and user-friendly. In his capable hands, the search for self-knowledge is not some mysterious algorithm but a profoundly practical and reachable goal.

— GREGG LEVOY, *author of Callings: Finding and Following an Authentic Life, and Vital Signs: The Nature and Nurture of Passion*

Like a skillful mapmaker, Michael lays out a clarion path for the reader to chart their own journey for change in however they need it--and we all need it. Equally applicable in life, love and career. CHANGES is a robust and useful guide and an important contribution to the field. A book of beauty and wisdom.

—MATTHEW MOSELEY, *communication strategist, author of Dear Dr. Thompson: Felony Murder, and the Last Gonzo Campaign. World record holder open water swimmer*

DEDICATION

To my parents, who encouraged my curiosity.

DOWNLOAD THE AUDIOBOOK FREE!

Just to say thanks for buying my book, I would like to give you the Audiobook version 100% FREE!

TO DOWNLOAD THE AUDIOBOOK GO TO:

http://www.arcintegrated.com/changes

CONTENTS

PART ONE - CHANGES

COGNITION

HEART

ACTION

NOURISHMENT

GUTS

CONTENTS

ENVIRONMENTS

SPIRIT

CHANGES IN MOTION

PART TWO - HOW TO FIND THE RIGHT HELPING PROFESSIONAL

PREFACE

Hello, and welcome to *CHANGES: The Busy Professional's Guide to Reducing Stress, Accomplishing Goals, and Mastering Adaptability.*

Ever wonder why things aren't going the way you planned? Why things are happening to you instead of you making them happen? Have you set out to create change in your life and then been drawn back to old patterns or ways of thinking that you were trying to avoid? Do you know what questions to ask that will ensure success in your personal and professional life again?

CHANGES will help you ask the right questions and get the answers you've been searching for as you strive toward creating the change you want.

Within these pages I encourage you to keep asking yourself three main questions.

- -

QUESTION 1: *What insights do I need and what specific actions should I take to create long-term change?*

- -

I have many clients, friends, family members, colleagues, and acquaintances with strong personal insight. Perhaps you fall into this category too. Sometimes even the most insightful among us reach for change and fall short. We can get so wrapped up in trying to understand where we are that we end up philosophizing, dialoguing, and goal setting ourselves to death. Spinning our wheels in this way diminishes our ability to create the life we want. It takes more than mere insight to get us across the finish line.

Insight is important. It sets out a clear path toward positive change. However, insight does not walk the path for us. The old adage, "knowledge is power," carries some truth, but there is so much more to empowerment than knowledge alone. If we don't apply what we come to understand, true change is limited.

We can have knowledge, wisdom, and understanding, but unless we apply it, we limit ourselves. Translating the knowledge into action is where real change happens. Imagine all the times you've understood what is best for you or had clarity about something, but didn't act. Not much changed, did it? Knowledge is powerful, but it is only part of the equation.

In every chapter of this book you'll find tried-and-true actions to take. If you do the work, you'll reap the rewards. If you're only interested in concepts, that's okay, you will find some interesting ones in the pages ahead. But don't get your hopes up about creating changes if your interest is merely academic or theoretical. If you are ready to apply the concepts to make lasting changes in your personal and professional life, then, congratulations, you are just the kind of reader I had in mind when I was writing this book!

The bridge from understanding to application is an important one to cross. This book navigates that crossing. Take responsibility for creating the change you seek. Mere insight or understanding will not get you there. You must do the work if you're going to make it across the bridge.

QUESTION 2: *How do my insights and actions improve my personal and professional life?*

Most of us spend the majority of our waking hours at work. So, what we focus on in our professional lives can influence how we spend our time and energy off the job as well.

As we continue to change, grow, and evolve as human beings, aspects of our lives rearrange themselves in order of current priority. We may change outlooks, let go of relationships, start new ones, eat less, drink more, eat more, drink less, and change what we decide is important from one chapter of our lives to the next.

Each of the personal habits, behaviors, and mental shifts we create, deliberately or inadvertently, impacts all other parts of our life. My hope is that you connect your personal development to improvement at work since the time spent on the job is such a big part of our lives.

Connecting self-exploration to your professional life means being honest about your work environment. Consider asking yourself: "Is this really where I want to be?" "Do I really believe there are no other options?" "How are my beliefs currently serving me?" "What am I willing to do to live the life I want?" Make no mistake, change-making is neither easy nor painless. Taking a good hard look at yourself may cause discomfort and lead to seeking answers to difficult questions.

Creating a life that you want doesn't necessitate leaving your job. Moving on to something new is just one potential *outcome. I only bring it up as a bit of a warning. Don't worry, there are many other outcomes related to professional development that can unfold as a result of self-exploration.*

- -

QUESTION 3: *How do the various parts of my life impact my ability to create the changes I want to make?*

- -

All of the facets of our lives are woven together. This interconnection is explained throughout the book. If you want to make true, sustainable change, understanding how the different aspects of your life influence each other will be crucial. We know intuitively that the different aspects of our lives are related. Our health, relationships, habits—these all influence one another . . . for better and for worse. Sometimes when we get attached to creating a specific change in one area of our life, we can lose track of this interconnectivity. For example, when considering how to manage your stress, your default might be to evaluate what's going on at work, and that makes sense. However, after more in-depth examination, you may uncover one or more of the following culprits:

- *You aren't getting enough sleep.*
- *You are on the fence about certain relationships.*
- *You don't exercise or aren't exercising enough.*
- *You are constantly experiencing conflict with loved ones.*
- *You feel stuck in your job and that nothing can be done to get you unstuck.*

You may discover as you chip away at the various stressors that they were actually the major contributors and that by addressing them, work is no longer as stressful. Even if work was the initial stressor, your ability to manage all of the contributing factors will still be necessary to resolve the issue. When we fail to trace one dimension of our lives to the network of others, we fail to get at the root of the problem.

There is a major advantage in looking at ourselves holistically. If we can see how all the different parts of our life connect, then the ability to influence each one greatly increases. I have seen this kind of personal macro-vision succeed in the lives of numerous organizational leaders and others I've worked with over the years. Whether you are trying to lose weight, change careers, improve your romantic relationship, or enhance your spiritual life, success hinges on adopting a holistic approach to guide you toward your goal. If you can examine what is truly helping or hindering your progress, it's also harder to live in denial or make excuses for not achieving what you want.

CHANGES explores seven aspects of your lived experience. These are the seven core dimensions of your life most fundamental to change making. If you examine each dimension individually and in relation to each other, then you can pinpoint your stumbling blocks. After all, it's just as important to find the land mines as it is to find the tools.

The success that stems from connecting the different parts of our experience transcends socio-economic status, occupation, age, and other such categorizations. Whether you are a corporate CEO or struggling to meet your basic needs, if you have the courage to examine yourself deeply and determine what lies behind your success and failure, you can truly develop. Exploring the seven dimensions in CHANGES will accelerate that growth.

WHAT NOW?

Do the homework. Take the time to explore ideas and experiment with them. Invest in yourself. If you aren't satisfied with the results, you will still find yourself in a different place from where you were, and you can alter your path once again. By experimenting with strategies, you learn what works for you, what doesn't, what is too easy, and what needs to be scaled back or further dissected. Taking action initiates growth.

Enjoy the Journey!

Michael

NOTE:

I want to acknowledge all the clients I've had the opportunity to work with over the years. I am honored to have been witness to some incredible change-making at the individual and organizational levels. Through working as a professional coach, organizational consultant, and psychotherapist, I have seen amazing courage, vulnerability, discipline, and resilience.

The stories in this book about clients have been altered to protect confidentiality. Some of these stories do not relate to one individual, but are composites of different individuals and encounters. I am grateful to every client I have worked with over the years for all the lessons learned.

In terms of this book's frame of reference, I should mention that while I have worked with clients from various cultural backgrounds, they have all lived in North America. In addition, I have taken part in cross-cultural exchange programs, studied abroad, and attended global conferences, but for the most part my educational background and training has been in the United States.

INTRODUCTION

MAINTAINING
HOLISTIC CHANGES

Like many people, Bill was challenged with shifting careers and building more productivity into his life. He wasn't in dire straits. He had an apartment, a girlfriend, and a job, but was unsettled. Furthermore, Bill had a sharp mind, a good education, many interests, and a kind heart. But Bill struggled to overcome things that weighed him down and kept him from reaching what he wanted. He was frustrated with his job, troubled by the conflict in his relationship, and concerned about his substance use.

We began working together to find insight into what was holding him back. Bill may remind you of people you have known or maybe even of yourself. I could certainly relate to a few of Bill's challenges.

When Bill started to examine the many facets of his life and understand how they were connected, he created momentum. He had the courage to examine the stories he had told himself and how they excused or reinforced the patterns in his life. Then Bill took action. He created more self-care practices and spent more time outdoors, where he longed to be. Consequently, he became more capable of managing stress. Better stress management led to a reduction of conflict in his romantic relationship. With less stress and conflict in his life, he was able to think more clearly and focus on shifting careers. He was able to connect the pieces of his life and acquire a greater sense of wholeness.

My philosophy on making and maintaining change encompasses a few core concepts, including these two:

1. The more we explore the complexity of who we are, as well how we relate to others, the more effective we become at creating long-term change.

2. The more we embrace the idea that each facet of our life is connected to all others, the more effective we become at creating long-term change.

I take a holistic approach in most things I do, including how I create lasting change. These ideas are based on my lived experience and over a decade of work with thousands of people through professional coaching, organizational consulting, and psychotherapy. I've worked with individuals from all walks of life and I've addressed a wide array of needs and desires. From owners of successful companies to those afflicted with severe and persistent mental health issues, everyone is looking for change. I have worked with the *"one percenters"* and with those just scraping by. I have been honored to partner with each and every one of my clients and to witness successful change in countless manifestations.

When I look back at the people and organizations I've worked with, I realize that the same connections we uncovered in their lives, through the process of creating positive change, I also found in my own life. The more we can connect the different parts of ourselves, the more successful we will be with any individual aspect.

Whether you are working with a coach, therapist, guru, or just moving through a process on your own, the ideas in this book are meant as a guide to make and maintain change.

When working toward change, particularly when it comes to goal achievement, reducing stress or adapting to challenging circumstance, it is important to consider all the aspects that may help, or hurt, your progress.

We are complicated creatures.

Creating the best version of ourselves is not only about thinking in a different way or practicing good habits. True and lasting change comes from evaluating all the parts and pieces of our human experience. When we align and look through all our different lenses, we get a clearer view of the truth and our likelihood of success skyrockets. Incidentally, I use the term *"success"* with caution. The success I am talking about comes from examining who you are, at the core level. The details of that success are up to you.

Take the example of Bill struggling with career transition and productivity. Upon looking through the different lenses—relationships, lifestyle choices, career choice, environment, self-care, belief systems, etc.—we see how each of these lenses affects the balance (or imbalance) of the others.

At our core, we all want to know how to create meaning in our world. To do so, we need to explore how we think, feel, act, and take care of ourselves. We also need to assess the strengths we have and with whom and what we surround ourselves.

I've created the CHANGES method to help you evaluate the different parts of yourself and discern what may be helping or hurting your progress.

Before we dive into this model, let me tell you about the process of creating the acronym, which followed the creation of the ideas.

Throughout my work as a professional coach, therapist, and organizational consultant I've spent thousands of hours exploring how people create change in their lives, both effectively and ineffectively. I've seen what stresses them out and what impacts their goal accomplishment as well as their failure. There are common threads in these processes.

There is already lots of information out there on how the various parts of our human experience impact each other. The biopsychosocial approach, for instance, is a model that looks at how biology, psychology, and social factors impact our general health.[1] I have spent a long time contemplating these questions:

- *What are the key elements that influence our ability to create the kind of change we want?*
- *What are the ruts, stumbling blocks, and pitfalls that show up, over and over, and keep us from reaching our goals?*
- *What are the various parts of ourselves that when integrated increase the likelihood of achieving our goals?*

In regard to all of these questions, I focused on three dimensions: how we think, how we act, and how we feel. Seems pretty intuitive. After long consideration, I realized that the dimensions that are the most common predictors of effective change making actually total seven. After I had these seven dimensions in mind, I did some serious spreadsheeting (imagine reverse-engineering an acrostic) and found an acronym that would serve as a mnemonic device.

I think it's important to clarify that most of the content of this book predates the gimmicky title. Let's be honest, acronyms work, and I want you to remember this stuff!

CHANGES represents:

C	**Cognition**
H	**Heart**
A	**Action**
N	**Nourishment**
G	**Guts**
E	**Environment**
S	**Spirit**

Each part of this acronym has important components to consider.

COGNITION - *The way we think*

Do you make decisions quickly, not quickly enough, issue strong judgments, think poorly of yourself or too highly perhaps? These are just a few ways to consider how you think. The important part is to critically evaluate your unique cognitive process as it relates to the changes you wish to create in your life. Both the way we think and what we focus on will impact our ability to change.

HEART – *How we feel*

Our emotions play a big part in our ability to succeed. If we remain confident, happy, grateful, curious, and positive, then we will have a greater chance of achieving change. If we are negative, depressed, sad, angry, reactive, or closed off from our emotions, we may have a harder time moving toward positive change. How we feel also relates to our relationships and how they impact our ability to change. Exploring our emotional self in all its variety helps us understand what emotions are influencing us, what we might be avoiding, and what we can do to realign.

ACTION – *Our habits and routines*

Thinking and feeling are important, but it is the actions we take that guide our thoughts and feelings. Our action, or inaction, plays a significant role in our ability to push toward our desired outcome.

NOURISHMENT – *How we take care of ourselves*

It is not news that the way we eat, how much we exercise, how well we sleep, and our general lifestyle all influence us from day to day and over the course of our lives. This influence is especially pertinent to the process of seeking and maintaining positive change. How we treat our body affects our motivation, energy, creativity, strength, and focus. Considering how we nourish ourselves is vital.

GUTS – *Our courage to seek out and act according to our most authentic self and truth*

When moving through a change, consider if you have the guts to ask the hard questions. Can you explore the important depths of yourself? The depths that include your strengths, but also your fears, insecurities, blind spots, and shadows? Can you do what's necessary to allow your most authentic self to come forward? Guts are required.

ENVIRONMENTS – *Whom and what we surround ourselves with*

Jim Rohn, the well-known author, personal development guru, sought-after speaker, and trainer has said, *"We are the average of the five people we spend the most time with."* When it comes to self-development, our environment goes beyond the people we choose to be around. Our environment includes our family members, workspace, city, and community, but it also involves other aspects, such as how our home looks and feels. For example, if you know you function at a higher level when things are organized, then keeping your living space clean and orderly may be an important factor in your growth and development.

SPIRIT – *Our belief systems and how we find and make meaning*

These are very important questions to consider. You can be a Christian, Muslim, Hindu, Jewish, Agnostic, Atheist, etc. No matter how you define yourself, your set of values contributes to your identity. Moreover, your sense of meaning and belief system informs how you go through the demanding process of creating change. Examining how your belief system plays out in your life is always helpful. How we frame the world and grapple with the *hows* and *whys* of our existence is a core component of how we interact, make decisions, and apply meaning. Considering this aspect of yourself in the change process is crucial.

~

All of these factors within the CHANGES system are important to address during any dedicated shift you are making, whether the subject is personal or professional. When I work with clients, this is part of the process I take them through.

> Unless we focus on all the potential areas that may be influencing our ability to make a change, we are leaving opportunity on the table.

It is important to remember that to realize any change you may be working toward takes time. Change works at its own particular pace. We'll explore this pace later in the book. For now, just be patient with yourself along the way.

INTRODUCTION ACTIVITY

Using the CHANGES acronym as a guide, develop a short outline of how each letter is reflected in your life. Write a few sentences about each. Then write down two personal strengths in each of the seven areas and two opportunities for growth. This exercise will develop some insight into how you can set yourself up for success in creating the change you desire, starting right now.

PART ONE
CHANGES

COGNITION

"Great minds discuss ideas, average minds discuss events, small minds discuss people."

—*Eleanor Roosevelt*

How we think about our lives and what we spend most of our time thinking about are two factors that influence our ability to change. Exploring the thoughts we get stuck on, our perceptions of situations, and how we process information all come into play when creating change.

Some people make monumental changes by shifting the way they think. Others are unable to move toward their goals because of their unbreakable tie to their current thinking patterns.

I encourage you to examine how you think and to determine honestly if it is helping or hurting your ability to seek the change you want in your life. This is not necessarily a book about positive thinking. Though you will explore some of your thought patterns and learn to modify them to create an optimistic space in which to create change, my goal is broader than that.

Seek the opportunity, not only in the new thought itself, but also in your ability to adapt to new ways of thinking. In other words, focus on adjusting the process, not the product. You can gain more momentum in change-making by evaluating how you think before you pursue the latest new idea. It's the difference between the pursuit of self-discovery and simply acquiring new information. Since you're reading this, kudos to you for your information gathering. With this book, you'll gain a greater ability to self-evaluate rather than just get some new tips and tricks.

Adapting your cognitive abilities can propel you to success. Experience the liberation of getting unstuck.

In this section, you'll have an opportunity to reflect on where you tend to focus and what occupies your thoughts. You'll detect patterns you have developed over time, assumptions you make, and the perspectives you've relied on for too long. Just like taking care of your eyes, perspectives need adjusting. Imagine sticking with the same eyeglass prescription that you had as a child. The world would appear fuzzy because your way of seeing it would be outdated. Challenge your status quo and let new ways of thinking sharpen your vision.

1

THE VICTIM OR
THE MASTER

The road from Arica, Chile, to Cochabamba, Bolivia, winds through terrain that is mostly arid, desolate, and rugged. After driving for hours, looking out into nothing, I would marvel when we came across one lonely house in the middle of nowhere. We'd stop to pick up someone waiting by the road, and I wondered, not only where they were headed, but also how they accessed food and water in such an isolated area. From my perspective, the whole situation seemed surreal.

A friend and I had started our journey in Santiago, Chile and slowly made our way up the coast. The bus ride through the desert eventually took us to the Bolivian border, near the Parinacota Volcano and Chungará Lake. The view of the dormant volcano rising above the lake in the middle of the desert is as stunning as it is unusual.

Spending so many hours on the bus, we had a chance to learn about our traveling companions. They had come from Germany, Australia, South Africa, and other places around the globe. There were about 40 of us in total; I think we were the only Americans on the bus. When we arrived at the border to cross from Chile into Bolivia, we exited the bus and in single file, headed into a small, two-door building. We were to enter through one door, speak to a border guard, and exit through the other door into the other country. Seemed easy enough.

As we made our way up the line, we became familiar with the routine. The guard assessed each traveler with an expression of stoicism tinged with irritation. He asked for their passport, gave it a quick glance, stamped it, and handed it back. Then the traveler would exit door number two and Voilà! Welcome to Bolivia.

I should note that the guard at the desk was flanked by two others standing behind him, each toting a very large automatic weapon. It's uncertain if the guns were just for show, but either way, they lost little of their power to intimidate.

When we stepped to the desk, we presented our passports to the seated guard. He opened them up, glanced at us, down at the passports, back at us, and then opened a drawer, tossed in both passports, and slammed it closed. He stared at us as if daring a reaction. As soon as we took the bait and started to formulate a question in Spanish, he motioned for us to move along. Our most polite efforts to reclaim our precious document only elicited an explanation that we would get them back at our next stop. Oruro was the next city in Bolivia on our journey, and it was here where we were supposed to change buses and head to our final destination of Cochabamba. It was another five-hour bus ride through the emptiness of Bolivia just to get to Oruro. Bear in mind that at this time, Bolivia was the second least industrialized country in South America. We were nervous, to say the least.

Given the firepower on the other side of the table and the uncertainty of what these guards might do if we didn't move along, we decided to cross our fingers and hope for the best.

24

We passed through door number two, climbed aboard the next bus with our fellow travelers, and headed out into the desert, passportless.

Looking back, I think my friend and I were each trying to play it cool, probably in support of each other. Later, in a more candid moment, we both admitted that we were barely holding it together. Adding a little more adrenaline to the mix, about two hours into our ride, in the middle of nowhere, the bus blew a tire. We were stranded on the side of the road while the repairs were made. At that point, I think something shifted. We didn't know what was going to happen, but we both realized that panicking was not going to get us anywhere.

I remember sitting on the side of the road, looking out into the distance, and feeling the heat of the sun on my skin. For a brief duration, I was able to be in the moment and reflect on the beauty in front of me. It was as if I was finally allowing something in that, consciously or not, I had been keeping out: gratitude.

I had just spent the last month traveling through South America experiencing a new environment, making wonderful new friends and connections, and learning of the cultural richness throughout the region. Furthermore, I was at the front end of another month of travel with a good friend. If I had been able to sustain this sense of presence, or if I had arrived at it earlier, I could have saved myself a lot of panic, anxiety, and fear.

A few hours later we arrived in Oruro. We found the building where we were meant to pick up our passports. The guys behind this desk were very friendly and had no guns. But neither did they have our passports. They apologized and told us to check back in a few hours.

At this point, panic set in again and dissolved all the serenity I had mustered sitting on the side of the road. Were our passports stolen? All communication thus far had been in Spanish. Did we misunderstand something in translation? Was it a case of cultural misunderstanding? All these questions and more ran through our minds and in and out of our conversation. We tried our best to keep the fear at bay. We had heard stories of the corruption in Bolivia from a friend who was a resident. Losing our passports and getting stuck in this small town in rural Bolivia was one thing, but knowing when and whom to bribe and when and whom not to was something else.

We did know one thing, we were starving. We had not eaten all day and were feeling it. We decided to see if we could find a place for pizza. Maybe some comfort food would do us well. And, as luck would have it, we found a pizzeria only about a ten-minute walk from where our passports were supposed to arrive.

Now why is this detail important, you might ask? Well, the pizza represents something much more important—letting go. The meal was a welcome distraction from fixating on the problem. It benefited us to take a few breaths, have some food, and gather our thoughts. Plus, truth be told, I eat when I'm stressed and pizza is my go-to food indulgence.

After we finished what was a decent attempt at a New York style thin crust pie, we felt a little better and could chat about contingency plans. When we checked back at the passport office, we braced ourselves for the worst. What was next? More automatic weapons? An arrest for not having proper identification? Some sort of bribe that we could not afford? As soon as we walked in, all eyes were on us, but it was because our passports had arrived!

Now what happened to our identities in the hours between our passports being confiscated and then landing back in our possession, I can't say. If you hear of another Michael Diettrich-Chastain out there in the world, please let me know.

When I look back at this experience, I take from it the lesson of identifying what was in my control and what was not. When we consider what happens to us, we always have a choice concerning how to perceive the situation, what to internalize, and how to act. It is in this decision-making process that one may succumb to something rather damaging and toxic: victimization.

What I want to say here is simple: we are not victims, ever. I realize this statement alone carries a lot of weight, and will probably evoke strong reactions, but let me elaborate. Of course, I recognize that there are all kinds of suffering in the world. Pain, misery, corruption, and injustice are real. But just like with every other experience in our lives, there are opportunities for positive change in our suffering. Even in the worst circumstances, there are opportunities for growth, education, and development. If we can recognize these opportunities, then we can transcend victimhood. Adverse situations may exist, but what I am referring to is *our perception of the world around us.* Our power lies in what we choose to take away from each situation and how we let it mold who we are. We have the choice to be The Victim or The Master.

We can see examples of this dichotomy—victimization vs. mastery—in both everyday life and the most horrific of ordeals. The famous story of Victor Frankl, as told in his book, *Man's Search for Meaning,* explores a man's fortitude while helplessly watching as a majority of those he knows and loves are killed in the concentration camp beside him.[2] He miraculously survives the camps and goes on to develop an entire therapeutic approach largely informed by his experience. His approach, Logotherapy, is based on the pursuit of meaning in one's life, which we play a role in creating.[3] Even in the most unfathomable circumstances, human resilience can prevail. This resilience is founded on perception. As Frankl himself recounts, his perception pushed him through a horrific situation, and his choice of response made him the master of it, not the victim.

You encounter opportunities to identify as either master or victim every day, such as when someone cuts in front of you in line or cuts you off on the highway; when a coworker gets mad for no apparent reason; when a family member avoids your calls; or when armed guards confiscate your passport. Fortunately, these are all invitations to look at the bigger picture. You get to decide if your perception will be one of victimization or one of mastery.

THE VICTIM AT WORK

When the victim is at work, *"life happens to you"*. When I went through the experience in Bolivia, I felt my own *"victim-at-work"* tendency kick in. It presented itself in questions such as, *"Why is this happening to me? Why are these guards doing this to us? What if there is nothing we can do to stop this?"* When the victim is at work, we are simply reacting to situations. In such a case, we assume we are powerless, that someone or something is dominating us. In my case, while the situation may have been somewhat out of our control, I still had a choice in how to respond.

Our passports had been taken. That was out of our hands, but I still had the choice of how to interpret the situation and what kind of identity I would take on in response. The crucial decision—to become The Victim or The Master—has to do with the response to what happened, not what actually took place. We may have in us a natural tendency to react in a certain way to situations. This quick reactivity tends to be defensive and often keeps us safe. However, to identify as a victim for too long or too frequently is dangerous. It leads to continued weakness, disempowerment, resentment, fear, and paralysis. Learn to recognize your default reactions (both natural and conditioned) and do something with them rather than be trapped by them.

THE MASTER AT WORK

When we address our sense of victimization, we get the opportunity to master a situation. In the case of the missing passports, instead of feeling defeated by the situation, I would have been better off asking myself the following questions:

- *What is in my control and what is not?*
- *In this moment, how much worse off am I, really?*
- *How does this offer me an opportunity to appreciate all that I do have?*
- *Most importantly, what kind of perception and identity am I choosing, and how is this serving me?*
- *What lessons can I learn from this?*

One of the lessons I took from my experience is to be more mindful and observant of my environment. I definitely could have checked into the border crossing process for that particular location where we crossed. It was a less frequented location, so I could have been more proactive in taking precautions. If you're laughing because of how obvious this seems, you're not alone.

Second, concerning how one's perception serves one's situation, the perception of the master is constructive, and that of the victim is destructive. By choosing to master my situation, I was able to forge ahead, let go of the negativity that surrounded the situation, and articulate the lessons learned. There are always lessons.

Ultimately, this event was a strong reminder that, regardless of circumstance, I get to choose what I do in response to circumstance. I could have made all sorts of decisions based on assumptions and emotions such as anger, indignation, self-pity, etc. Instead, I chose to evaluate what could be gained and how to let go.

THE 4 R'S – *A Tool for Recognizing the Victim or the Master*

You may have already heard of the concept of React or Respond. The way I think of it is that reaction is your automatic/limited thought, statement, or action. It is involuntary. A response, by contrast, is a choice. A response is the statement or action made after greater awareness arrives. For example, your significant other makes a request you don't appreciate after you've had a long, hard day, and your first impulse is to dismiss them, get angry, or maybe just grab a beer and head to the living room (reaction). The alternative is to take a breath, cultivate a question for them concerning what they need, or calmly explain your situation so that you and your significant other can discuss what needs to get done while being mindful of each other's needs (response).

That all sounds fine and dandy, right? The problem with this concept is that it may be too cerebral. The integration of awareness is missing. Unless we apply what we understand, that understanding is fruitless. This is another excellent example of how awareness of a concept will yield minimal impact on true change.

The way to integrate an awareness of how you are either reacting or responding to a situation is to introduce two other R's—Resistance vs Relaxation. Even though this concept may sound new to you, I promise this is familiar territory. Do this quick experiment:

Think of a time when you have definitely reacted. Maybe the barista made your drink incorrectly and you were already late. Perhaps your boss barked an order at you or criticized you in a manner that was rude and uncalled for. Or the time your neighbor's tree fell in your yard and you told them how you really felt about their stupid haircut.

Once you have your scenario in mind, remember the sensations in your body. Possible sensations you may recall are: heat, heaviness, tension, or other areas of *"resistance."* When your body is in a state of resistance, it's hard to come up with a thoughtful *"response."* We have all experienced resistance as a sensation in our life before, and we have felt stuck in a reaction mode because of it.

Now, think of a time when you had to make a decision, but felt more at ease. You were probably able to think things through clearly or perhaps you had a productive conversation with someone about the decision. Remember how your body felt in this state. Sensations you may have noticed in this case may include a sense of fluid motion, a lightness, and a soft or relaxed feeling. This is the state we are in when we are able to respond rather than react. When our body and mind are in a relaxed state we have the flexibility of choice.

Of course, the next question is, *"How do I get there?"* The answer, as you may have guessed, is practice. Having an insight into how your body feels is a start. Understanding the link between how you feel physically and how you choose to respond is a gateway to shifting patterns in your own behavior.

Next time you are faced with a situation where you feel anger, hate, pity, self-doubt, or anything else unpleasant, ask yourself a question, *"Am I The Victim or The Master?"*

CHAPTER 1 ACTIVITY

There is constant opportunity to shift your standpoint from victim to master. The subtlety of our perceived victimization can be the most damaging because it is often the most consistent. Here is a chance to create, keep track of, and bring awareness to change! Start to log your shifts in perception. The more frequently you track your actions and shifts, the easier it will become. This activity will take two weeks.

WEEK ONE

Start by dividing a page into fourths. Label the first section, "*Situation,*" the second, "*Victimized Reaction,*" the third, "*Masterful Response,*" and the final one, "*Victories.*" In the "*Situation*" section, write down situations that forced you to decide between playing the victim and playing the master. In the "*Victimized Reaction*" section, log examples of how you reacted to situations when you took the identity of the victim. In the area labeled "*Masterful Response,*" write down an alternative response, one that would have made you master of the situation. Do this activity daily.

WEEK TWO

In the area labeled "*Victories,*" log instances when you actually did offer a masterful response. These will be times when you resisted taking on the role of victim, when you applied your heightened self-awareness, and took actions or made decisions that reflected the person you aspire to be. After some practice, you'll find yourself jotting down more *"Victories"* than *"Victimized Reactions."* You can always circle back to this activity and/or do it for longer periods of time if you need more practice.

EXAMPLE

Situation	The barista took too long to make my double espresso I really needed before an important meeting I was running late for.	Partner yelled at me for not picking up dog food at the store.
Victimized Reaction	I told her, *"Hurry up, I don't have all day."*	
Masterful Response	I could have taken three deep breaths and remembered that she has a story I'm not aware of, one that may affect her efficiency.	
Victories		Instead of yelling back, I calmly asked how she was doing in an attempt to understand her better. Then we made an agreement about how to move forward and set boundaries for communicating with each other more respectfully.

2

BUILDING
MOTIVATION
TO CHANGE

When looking at building motivation to change, you first need to tap into your truest sense of self. Every person's motivation to change is unique. We find true motivation in the intersection of what we are excited about (passion), what we find meaningful (purpose), what we have done (experience), and what we are good at (talent). The process starts with identifying where these areas uniquely intersect for you.

I once read an article on how, in just twenty minutes, you can find your true calling by tapping into what you deeply connect with. It was a powerful writing exercise that basically had you brainstorming ideas until you wrote one down that moved you to tears. Discerning what truly moves you is the kind of motivation that can help you make successful change.

That said, what truly motivates or moves us may not be obvious. I was once chatting with a client (we'll call him Harry) about what kept him engaged and motivated in his work. He was quick to respond that he was motivated by making money. We discussed the importance of money and specifically what he liked to do with his. He mentioned his passion for mountain biking and photography, but above all, he said, he loved traveling. After more conversation, we discovered that for him money was, at best, a conduit for the freedom and adventure he experienced every time he traveled.

In other words, an itch to explore played a greater role in his life than did economic concerns. When I asked Harry if he would take a job that offered more money but less vacation time he said he probably wouldn't. This surprised him, given his initial response about being motivated primarily by money.

I tell this story because understanding what really motivates us takes some serious introspection. You can write down intentions, mark your calendar, join a support group, and a million other things in the pursuit of your goals, but if you don't have a true understanding of yourself, then you probably won't get to where you want to go. Working toward change through authentic motivation will lead you to reach goals faster and more easily. If you haven't yet identified the biggest driving factor behind the changes you desire, then the activities below will help you explore who you are and what motivates you.

Exploring your preconceived notions about motivation and change is a great first step. You'll have the chance to gain new insight in this chapter, but more importantly, you'll learn how to apply this insight.

FOUR TIPS ON BUILDING MOTIVATION NECESSARY FOR CHANGE

1. EXPLORE YOUR STRENGTHS

In assessing what motivates you, consider your talents. We are drawn to do things we are good at. According to a 2009 article in *The Journal of College and Character*, research shows character strengths are linked to important aspects of social and individual well-being.[4] Unclear about your strengths? Consider asking a person from five different areas of your life what they view as your strongest qualities. Yes, this may sound a bit intimidating, but I have witnessed firsthand the value of this exercise time and again. Sometimes, those close to us see us more clearly than we see ourselves. Ask family members, partners, friends, work colleagues, and members of your faith community. The inventory may bring up talents that you never noticed or considered a strength.

2. IDENTIFY WHAT ENERGIZES YOU

For three weeks take note of every time you feel excited, energized, or strongly driven in a particular area. Be open to these feelings in all areas of your life and times of the day. No matter where and when these moments occur Write. Them. Down.. After you have a list of experiences, see what themes emerge. These themes may be areas that you can refer to when building motivation to change a particular area of your life.

3. TAKE A STAND

Take a stand about those things that are truly meaningful to you. Consider which aspects of your life you pay particular attention to. What do you have a strong opinion about? What are your strongest passions? If it's not obvious to you what your passions are, use the inventory from step number one to identify them. Understanding what you are passionate about will help you build authentic motivation.

4. GET ADDITIONAL RESOURCES

Still having trouble determining how to create authentic motivation? Consider looking into some kind of assessment tool or working with a professional coach. Taking an assessment can be a valuable place to start evaluating your unique strengths and challenges. For example, an assessment tool called Values Index explores one's unique motivation profile based on seven primary dimensions. For more information about this tool, visit www.arcintegrated.com/coaching. This tool is a great resource for uncovering your truest motivation.

REPS

Reaching your goals can be tough, we all know that. But what about the particulars? How do you muster the resolve to continue with a goal after being on the verge of quitting? How do you cultivate the faith required to convince yourself that your hard work is moving you toward fulfillment instead of toward failure and frustration? How do you manage to stay motivated after you've reached the first part of the goal and celebration mutates into complacency? Staying motivated to reach new goals may take Reflection, Evaluation, Persistence, and Significance (REPS). During our progress toward a goal, we practice something over and over again; we are doing *"reps"* (short for repetitions). Just like in any change-making process, repetition of behaviors creates sustainability.

WHY REPS IS IMPORTANT

Reflection – It's important to look at what got you to where you are and what lies ahead. Reflecting on progress toward a goal can be an effective way to clarify where you have come thus far and to foster a sense of accomplishment that will drive you forward. This examination will also help you identify what has kept you motivated, what has gotten in your way of accomplishing goals in the past, and, more specifically, which of your cognitive and behavioral patterns have helped or hindered your progress. This process may also lead to new goal setting, which is another benefit.

Evaluation – It's important to be clear about the details of the goal. What motivates you toward the goal, what do you gain from it, and what does it mean to you? Make sure that your progress toward realization is evident and measurable. You might consider writing down, voice recording or otherwise capturing answers to some or all of the following questions. Why you are starting this goal? What's important about it? How do you imagine you will feel when you finish? What are the exact steps to completion? How can you be held accountable? As well as any other questions that may bring to light details that are important to consider, including strategies to avoid potential pitfalls. For instance, if your goal is to eat healthier and you know that your favorite donut place is on the way home from work every day, you might consider changing routes as part of your strategy. It's often the missed details of a goal that trip us up along the way.

Persistence – Accomplishing a difficult task often takes time. It certainly requires lots of effort. Stay strong, continue to work hard, dig deep, and certainly don't quit something because you think you have mastered it. Change perspectives and learn how to bring the curiosity and enthusiasm of a beginner to the task. There is a Zen Buddhist concept that may be valuable to consider—*Shoshin*. Roughly, this translates to *"beginner's mind."* An attitude of openness and curiosity helps in cultivating Shoshin.

Significance – Staying motivated may be easier if you keep in mind the significance of your goal. Consider the significance not only for you, but also for others who are important to you, your community, and humanity in general.

If you are struggling to maintain a clear conception of your goal's significance, you might consider asking others. Meaning, asking others what it would mean to them to have you accomplish your goal. For example, asking your significant other, children, or people in your community what they think about you completing the goal. In addition, if you've written down a previous plan for this goal (see Evaluation section), consider circling back to remind yourself why it was so important to you in the first place. When driving toward your goal, it is not uncommon get lulled into a stupor from the monotony of the practice and lose the full impact of crossing the finish line. The reality is that no one can be "*on*" all the time. Passion naturally fluctuates. During those times when passion for your goal is waning, consider re-reading the note you wrote down or the recording you made at the beginning of the process to reignite your enthusiasm. This evaluation can also lead to consider whether or not to continue with the goal. Be honest with yourself.

REPS IN ACTION

- -

1. *Identify what other goals or sub-goals have been accomplished, how they were accomplished, and how this can lead to setting and accomplishing new goals. (Reflection)*

- -

Goals are rarely permanent. Having a sense of accomplishment when completing a goal is a wonderful thing, but this should not be confused with a license to rest on your laurels. To stay motivated around progress, it may be important to consider what new opportunities exist now that your goals are accomplished. There are always new ways to grow and new goals to achieve.

----

2. Identify what is truly important. (Evaluation)

When we set goals for ourselves it is helpful to identify what is truly meaningful to us. Once accomplished, goals may reveal new meaning and value in our lives. Furthermore, accomplishment in and of itself may open up new meaning to us. Asking ourselves what is truly important with every accomplished goal can direct us to the next steps in the overall process.

----

3. What are the pros and cons of quitting? (Evaluation)

Making lists is very important. You may be surprised to discover that something so simple can be so useful! Oftentimes, when we write out pros and cons, it can help us see the bigger picture and assess our decisions more clearly. When considering whether or not to keep moving toward a goal, it can be particularly helpful to see the options written out in front of you. Evaluate the consequences of continuing to work for it and the consequences of shifting focus.

----

4. How can you learn from this situation, even when you think you've mastered it? (Persistence)

Sometimes we believe we have mastered a task when it is no longer challenging. Without a challenge we are liable to simply go through the motions, lose interest, and turn away *from our work before the end goal is reached. Repetition can also become tedious and ultimately discouraging. However, there are ways to keep curiosity and motivation thriving in such situations. Here are a few questions to ask yourself:*

- *How would I teach this activity to a beginner?*
- *How can I shift my perception to gain a better understanding of it?*
- *Is there a way I can continue toward my goal, but vary the work so it feels less repetitive and boring?*
- *How can I add a challenge in order to keep moving forward and stay engaged?*
- *If this is a personal development goal, how can it be applied to a professional goal or vice versa?*

- -

5. Who else benefits from the continued work? (Significance)

- -

When looking at goals and continuing to work toward them, it can be easy to think only about ourselves. One strategy to stay motivated toward accomplishing goals is to consider others. Whether they are professional goals or personal development goals, there are always other people involved, either directly or indirectly. Ask yourself the following, "How does my decision impact others, both in the short term and long term?"

CHAPTER 2 ACTIVITY

Where do you find motivation?

Use the following steps to uncover your motivation. See the instructions in the previous pages to work through each of the steps.

Step 1: Create an inventory of strengths.

Step 2. Take note of your excitement!

Step 3. Take a stand!

Step 4. Get additional resources.

WHAT'S YOUR STORY?

My grandmother hosts an annual party called *"Christmas in July,"* which is often held in August. No, I don't know why. The day of the party there is rarely a dull moment, even during the preparations. I am always reminded of how entertaining the hustle and bustle can be: deciding by committee who is going to make which dish, who will take on which cleaning chore, who is going to pick up the ice, which glass (water, red wine, white wine, etc.) goes where . . . In addition to family, the guest list includes friends who have been so close for so long that they feel like family. These are mostly friends I grew up with who have stayed in the area and now attend with families of their own. The party is especially important to me because it gives me the chance to reconnect with these loved ones whom I don't get to see as often as I'd like now that I live five states away.

I grew up in the Midwest between Milwaukee and Chicago on a horse farm that borders a beautiful, wooded state park. The farm was a horse boarding business during most of my childhood. Our clients would rent stalls and pasture from us and we would take care of their horses. It was and still is an environment filled with activity, fun, and lots of work.

If you haven't been to the Midwest, then you should go. Yes, I know, it's not on the way to anything, but there are lots of pockets of entertaining cities, beautiful countryside, and friendly people. If you do go, don't go in the winter unless you are partial to deep snow and bone chilling wind. The summers are beautiful.

That's one glimpse into my life. One piece of my story. Every time I return home, I recall how much I have to be grateful for. And I am particularly grateful for all of the values that I associate with home. The following are a few values that stand out:

WORK ETHIC

I spent a fair amount of my early years shoveling horse shit and probably just as much time complaining about it. The never-ending piles, the never-ending calls to get back out to the barn, the rough weather that added insult to injury . . . But now, all these years later, I'm grateful for the experience. Funny how time changes perspective. Looking back, I realize that some of my most tedious chores held many important lessons. Today, whenever I return to the farm, I am glad that I can still contribute. In the fall/winter, there's chopping wood for the stove. In the summer and spring, there are animals to feed, outbuildings calling for upkeep, and acres of landscaping that require tending. It may seem counterintuitive, but I look forward to these tasks. Growing up on a farm—where there is always something to do—taught me the value of hard work. A strong work ethic is a common trait in all the role models I have had over the years, especially in those who are truly successful. Hard work pays off. Always.

HUMOR

My friends and family are hilarious . . . At least, we think so. If there is such a thing as a particularly Midwestern sense of humor, I find it to be sarcastic, dry, and mildly self-deprecating. I'm not sure that my description distinguishes it from other regional senses of humor, but I know it when I encounter it, and it's close to my heart. Frankly, it's another reason I visit home. My grandmother, the Christmas in July party hostess, is funny without even trying to be. If you were to meet her, it's likely you would consider her the kindest person you'd met in a long while. But just go and upset her Christmas in July agenda, and you'll see another side. Fair warning, it's intense. She once bit a police officer. But that's another story. Thankfully for her and the officer, no major injuries or charges ensued.

Grandma aside, perhaps, my family rolls with punches by finding the humor in both life's ups and its downs. My aunt is a great catalyst for this. Her keen observations of the irony of situations or of people's quirks and baffling behaviors somehow keep us all on our toes and in good spirits. As my family masterfully demonstrates to me every time I'm with them, humor is invaluable in de-stressing, changing perspective, and shifting the tone on your worst day. It's all too easy to become too analytical, serious, and defensive. I owe a debt of gratitude to all my friends and family who can always make me laugh, cheer me up, or convince me to take myself less seriously.

NATURE

Growing up, I spent many hours in the state park that borders our farm. I wandered in the woods, build forts, hiked around, looked for animals, rode bikes with friends, and just enjoyed being outside. I remember going for walks in the woods as a teenager to escape some of the angst, drama, and stress that often accompany those years. Now when I return home, I still go on walks in the woods for exercise or to de-stress. There is also the added bit of nostalgia now.

For me, being in a rural environment is more relaxing. Even though my family's farm is filled with work, it is also filled with a sense of deep connection to the elements. Taking a break from the hustle, traffic, and commerce that defines city life is a great way to gather new energy. It can be so easy to get swept away with the to-do lists, the constant technological distractions, and rapid pace of life that we all-too-frequently excuse as normal. Making contact with nature allows me to step back, take a deep breath, and ground myself.

These are a just a few aspects of my story for which I am grateful.

So, now you might ask, *"What does gratitude or storytelling have to do with creating change or reaching goals?"*

Let me explain.

You always have a choice. Regardless of how chaotic, dysfunctional, traumatic, or otherwise negative you think your experience was growing up, you have a choice to shift your perception and to do so without stumbling into wishful thinking or delusion. You can choose to frame your experience in any way you'd like. You'll have an opportunity to practice acting on this shift at the end of the chapter.

In my work as a coach, organizational consultant, and therapist, I have seen people make changes in their life that seemed nearly impossible beforehand. I have seen wisdom and insight come out of the most infuriating, heartbreaking, and seemingly hopeless personal stories.

While we may be shaped by our stories, we also have the opportunity to reshape them and, by extension, ourselves. This is where perception comes in. By acknowledging our story and the lessons within it, we create a new story, one that reinforces our strengths instead of pointing to our weaknesses or victimization. Consider what you have learned and how you have grown rather than how you have suffered. Processing pain is valuable, don't get me wrong, but there are consequences to letting it continue to shape you. This simple shift in perception will change your life.

What lessons can you learn from your story? For which aspects of your story are you most grateful?

CHAPTER 3 ACTIVITY

Your turn! Time to write down a few significant stories from your life, as I have. I suggest three short accounts. These could be simple memories, significant life events, or poignant moments that stand out.

After you've completed each story, write down three lessons you take from it. Remember that it's important to explore how each story may mean something different to you now than it did back then. Recounting and reflecting on these stories allow you to build the muscle of perspective.

HEART

"If your emotional abilities aren't in hand, if you don't have self-awareness, if you are not able to manage your distressing emotions, if you can't have empathy and have effective relationships, then no matter how smart you are, you are not going to get very far."

—Daniel Goleman

You are not your emotions. Our emotions can be our greatest companions and our most ruthless masters. They can lead us to great heights of bliss and into depths of unimaginable pain. When making a life change, our emotions play a significant role in our success and stagnation.

While we are influenced by our emotions, we can choose how much we listen to their constant call. We can implement specific strategies to manage our emotions effectively, rather than become enslaved by them. Emotions serve us better when they bring us closer to reality than when they dictate reality.

If you feel that your emotions have the reins, you need to understand that you can take back control. You can direct your life the way you want it to go. The narratives dictated by our emotions can be rewritten. We can recover from pain, heartache, death, and so much more. We are resilient.

A better understanding of our emotional selves can offer us incredible insight into our wisdom, connection, empathy, and stressors. If you are willing to be brave and embrace all aspects of your emotional self, you can create positive change in a new way.

This section explores some of the ways emotion influences the change process. You'll also find specific strategies you can implement to develop a more effective emotional self. Exploring our emotions can be overwhelming at times. Be patient, be brave, and let your heart remain open.

4

EMOTIONAL INTELLIGENCE – PROFESSIONAL AND PERSONAL

W hat is emotional intelligence? Emotional intelligence is the ability to understand, influence, and communicate emotions, both yours and those of others. That's a short definition, at least.[5] Leading authority, Daniel Goleman, expands the term to include four areas of emotional intelligence: self-awareness, self-management, social awareness/empathy, and relationship management.[6] There are other understandings of the term, but Goleman's basic framework is well-accepted.

The measure of emotional intelligence is referred to as emotional quotient (EQ), though the terms are often used interchangeably. For the purposes of this chapter, we'll use the term EQ going forward.

Fortunately for us, EQ can be developed, unlike your intelligence quotient (IQ), which is relatively stable over time. There are many ways to improve our EQ. As research continues to mount, a strong relationship between EQ and success in the business world has emerged from the data.

For instance, according to *Talent Smart*, which tested 34 important workplace skills, it was found that emotional intelligence is one of the strongest predictors of peak performance in all types of jobs.[7] It appears that EQ is a key component in team functionality, leadership, communication, among other areas. In my experience, I have witnessed clients develop EQ and practice it across all areas of life.

HOW TO IMPROVE EMOTIONAL INTELLIGENCE

Often, organizations will solicit executive or leadership coaches to work with employees to build emotional intelligence. These coaches employ assessment tools that help cultivate empathy and enhance understanding of the strengths, blind spots, and stressors of individuals and teams. The EQ training that consultants and coaches provide is another way to improve the overall performance of the organization, from the individual to teams, across all departments. Leaders benefit greatly from building EQ skills.

THREE WAYS LEADERS CAN IMPROVE EQ:

1. **Build empathy for employees** by exploring strengths and specific leadership styles and determining how these styles can complement others within the organization. For instance, consider educating yourself on a model called

Situational Leadership.[8] This model provides a simple strategy to understand the various ways to lead particular employees. The idea is that leaders take into account an employee's experience and motivation as they pertain to a particular job, task, or project and then apply the leadership style that best fits that particular profile. For example, an employee that has limited experience with a certain task but is highly motivated may respond well to a leadership style that is more directive and hands-on.

2. **Improve EQ as a leader** by practicing more self-care, self-reflection, and self-awareness. This may sound counterintuitive, but focusing on self-care (see more in chapter 11) allows us to reduce stress, be less reactive, and handle pressure with more grace. Self-reflection and self-awareness build our capacity to understand our own strengths and weaknesses and recognize our blind spots, without which, both EQ and leadership suffer. As a leader, it may be challenging to receive feedback, communicate effectively, and understand others' needs without putting aside time to attend to your own needs.

3. **Explore communication styles** with the goal of understanding your own strengths and overcoming your challenges in how you communicate with employees. There are specific assessments you can utilize that explore how you communicate in great depth. My firm, Arc Integrated, uses an assessment called The Advanced Insights Profile to help teams and leaders examine their unique ways of communicating and understand how their differences can actually be leveraged to their advantage. This examination

leads to greater empathy, better organizational practices, and clearer communication within the business as well as with customers.

To some, developing one's self as an emotionally intelligent leader may sound like too much work for too little reward. To others, it may come across as psychobabble. But more and more evidence suggests that there are major benefits to cultivating emotional intelligence. Raising EQ boosts organizational performance across the board, from productivity to rapport to leadership.

The Graduate School of Applied and Professional Psychology at Rutgers University assembled an excellent argument for the close relationship between emotional intelligence and business success, offering 19 examples of how EQ contributes to the bottom line.[9] For example, in a 1990 article in *The Journal of Marketing* it was found that a store manager's ability to manage stress directly related to a retail chain's success as measured by net profits.[10] In another example, a manufacturing plant whose workers had recently received emotional intelligence training saw a 17 percent increase in production.[11] According to a sourcebook of three decades of research by The Center for Creative Leadership, there is evidence to show that the primary causes for derailment in executive careers involve deficits in emotional intelligence.[12] These deficits include difficulty working in teams, problems with interpersonal relations, and challenges handling change.

Being an emotionally intelligent leader doesn't mean losing track of specific goals or directives. It also doesn't mean ignoring data that often drives executive decisions. In essence, possessing high emotional intelligence may simply mean being adaptable in how we engage with others.

Leadership is certainly not limited to the organization. We can improve our leadership skills as individuals by understanding how we interact as friends, partners, and family members. Building our own leadership skills by increasing our EQ is always a valuable pursuit. Life presents plenty of opportunities to practice how we behave with those in our professional and personal circles.

Here are some aspects of your personal life that will benefit from improved leadership skills and increased EQ.

DEFINING LEADERSHIP BEYOND THE ORGANIZATION

Leadership can be distilled to a simple definition: guiding and influencing others. We are all leaders in some realm of our lives. Whether at work, at home, or in our community, we have the chance to lead. Each of us affects those around us in all situations. And whether this effect is positive or negative depends on our thoughts and behaviors as we walk through all aspects of life.

THE EMOTIONALLY INTELLIGENT LEADER AS A PARENT

Parents are leaders in the household. Everything they do has significance, as well as everything they don't do. They guide and influence their children with every action and inaction. Their communication style makes an impact. Parents have an important and unique opportunity to contribute to the foundation of children's emotional and communicative development.

Emotional Intelligence is crucial to how we communicate and collaborate in raising children. The ramifications of parenting with high emotional intelligence are evident in children as they grow into independent adults. They carry their deeply instilled behaviors with them into the world. Consider the consequences of leading in your household with high emotional intelligence.

Teaching children to communicate their feelings at an early age helps them develop their own emotional intelligence. How you frame emotional expression is important too. Effectively communicating a wide spectrum of emotions as a parent can help children understand their own feelings. It also teaches them how to express different emotions in healthy ways appropriate to each. It should be noted that the hiding or shaming of emotions often has negative consequences on EQ.

Guiding children in the expression of their emotions and helping them to recognize emotions in others helps them build strong EQ. It also gives them a deeper understanding of collaborating and communicating with high emotional intelligence at an earlier, more impressionable age.

To teach children how to express themselves and recognize emotion in others is just as important as their academic education, perhaps even more so. Given its implications on careers and relationships, EQ is clearly a crucial part of personal development.

The risks of failing to develop emotional intelligence are great for individual, family, and community. For example, according to a 2007 study cited in *The Journal of Personality and*

Individual Differences, which explored EQ in almost 8,000 individuals, higher emotional intelligence is associated with better physical health.[13] Research continues to be published, but if we can reasonably assume that there is a strong relationship between EQ and health, then shouldn't this drive us toward focusing on EQ as a non-negotiable component of good parenting? Effective communication skills, coupled with emotional literacy, are influential factors across all of our relationships, both intimate and professional.

THE EMOTIONALLY INTELLIGENT LEADER AS A ROMANTIC PARTNER

As a quick preface, it's important that I clarify what I mean by *"good leadership,"* especially in the context of a romantic partnership. Good leadership (in any context) is neither domineering, nor inflexible. Good leaders are those who take responsibility, demonstrate excellent communication skills, show a willingness to take feedback, and work to inspire rather than to instill fear. Good leaders are willing to show vulnerability. These attributes are essential for healthy romantic relationships.

A well-developed ability to understand ourselves, communicate, and empathize with others becomes particularly important in regard to our significant others. But how does one lead with these qualities? Building a strong connection and leading with emotional intelligence in relationships can be expressed in a number of ways. Consider these tips to practice emotional intelligence with your partner:

- *Practice showing empathy, being curious, and asking questions. Instead of making assumptions about your partner, remain committed to truly understanding his/her feelings, perspectives, and states of being. When you notice judgement creep in, take a step back, and attempt to reframe matters so that the focus is on him/her, not your knee-jerk reaction.*
- *Explore your own assumptions and feelings and be willing to share this exploration. A willingness to be vulnerable with your partner is vital to a healthy relationship. Offering an invitation to connect on a deeper level is a strategy shared by strong leaders as well as those with high EQ.*

THE EMOTIONALLY INTELLIGENT LEADER AS A FRIEND

Evaluating friendships is something many of us put off because it requires a level of honesty that can lead to uncomfortable revelations. Your first challenge is to clarify what kinds of friendships you want to cultivate. The second, and often more difficult challenge, is to define how you want your current friendships to evolve.

Being an emotionally intelligent leader in friendships doesn't entail guiding friends' behavior. Being a leader is about setting an example, inspiring, establishing clear boundaries, and living in congruence with your own values and principles. It is possible to demonstrate these leadership attributes in any relationship at any time. We can be the model of what kind of relationship we want.

Consider these tips for being an emotionally intelligent leader in a friendship:

- *Understand your own boundaries, values, and principles, and be willing to communicate them. Some people may be taken aback, but if you are clear about who you are and where you stand, your message will resonate, especially with the kinds of friends who most closely identify with you.*

- *Communicate the kind of friendship that you expect in return by modeling the dynamic you wish to create. This means that if you want a relationship to include vulnerability, direct and authentic feedback, humor, and maybe even a push for continued development, be the first one to offer these elements. However, in talking about friendship dynamics I don't mean to imply that the matter is so explicitly transactional. The point is that if you want to emphasize a certain dynamic in the relationship, be the one to initiate the change. Communicating clearly with friends about your own expectations, feelings, and experiences is a sign of strong EQ. This kind of communication will help to build stronger connections in current friendships and future ones as well.*

- *Be curious about the goings on in the lives of your friends. When in conversation, listen carefully and try to respond with genuine enthusiasm. Sincere curiosity will strengthen your connections and impress upon your friends that you are invested in what they have to say. If you repeatedly find yourself disengaged in a particular person's company, then perhaps the dynamics of that relationship need to change or maybe the friendship has simply run its course. I'm not recommending that you go cutting people out of your life left and right, but evaluating things can be helpful. Remember to remain curious about who they are, the messages they have, and the dynamic of your relationship.*

CHAPTER 4 ACTIVITY

As you've read, there are plenty of opportunities to improve and practice EQ. Now is your chance to put it to work.

Track your emotional intelligence development across your various life domains. Note what is successful and consider how to translate each success into other areas of your life. For instance, if you've been able to build empathy for those at home, consider how you can transfer that empathy for those at work. Write down your stories and track the development of your own EQ across the following areas of your life.

Emotional Intelligence at Work

Emotional Intelligence as a Parent/Child

Emotional Intelligence in Romantic Partnership

Emotional Intelligence in Friendship

5

TRUSTING YOUR INTUITION

Oxford defines intuition as *"The ability to understand some-thing instinctively, without the need for conscious reasoning."*[14] Today, the notion of intuition is greeted with much confusion, debate, and skepticism. At the very least, it raises a whole host of questions." For instance, how do you differentiate between what your heart says and an old pattern of behavior? What is the difference between intuition and fear? These are questions I've fielded frequently in my career and attempted to answer in my own life. In this chapter, I want to offer some tools I find helpful in exploring when to trust intuition.

First, let's look at some research on intuition. According to a study by researchers at University of Iowa College of Medicine published in *Science* magazine, subjects often relied on intuition before relying on conscious knowledge even when solving complex problems in different scenarios.[15] One scenario involved a card game in which participants had to choose from two decks, one stacked with opportunities to win, the other rigged to lose. Reaching for the bad deck elicited a physical response from subjects (their palms started sweating). This physical response occurred before participants reported a conscious awareness about which deck was stacked in their favor.

Another study looked at intuition as it relates to major life decisions, such as buying a car. It concluded that people who trust their intuition from the outset often end up happier than those who analyze decisions and end up deciding against their own intuition.[16] It should be noted that consensus on the subject has yet to be reached. Scientists, especially psychologists, continue to debate the nature of intuition.

Some believe intuition comes from the reptilian part of the brain, which taps into an unconscious awareness of danger. Without going into too much detail, this is the part of the brain that is responsible for the *"fight, flight, or freeze"* reaction. Others regard intuition as tapping into the unconscious and processing stored information that is perhaps difficult or near impossible for our conscious mind to access.[17] Others consider intuition as a way to tap into a more esoteric, universal knowledge. According to this perspective, intuition is a path to a greater truth.

Putting the debate aside, the overwhelming majority of articles, papers, and books written on the subject do at least agree on one thing: your intuition is worth listening to for a variety of reasons.

I often live by my intuition, perhaps too much so at times. I have allowed my intuition to guide decisions on career, relationships, where to live, and many other things. Almost always, I'm glad I listened to my gut. Regardless of how much you decide to listen to your intuition, taking a closer look at it will be valuable. Without examining our intuition, we forfeit one of the greatest tools available to us.

When I was considering graduate schools, I researched many programs, as is usual for the process. I finally landed on a school in the mountains of North Carolina. I was drawn to its unique program curriculum, especially its emphasis on Body Centered Therapy. (I'll elaborate on the importance of the mind/body connection in the *"Nourishment"* section of the book.) The stunning beauty of the mountains of Western NC was definitely a draw for me too. After some additional research, I realized that the recommended deadline for application had passed. Applicants had been admitted and there was already a waiting list. At this point, the logical option was to wait until the following year to apply. Especially since my GRE (a test most graduate schools require) scores were just below the minimum threshold.

But the pull the school had on me convinced me that this was *supposed* to be. So, following my intuition, I applied for the program right then anyway. I followed up by arranging a visit to the campus for a face-to-face introduction with professors and administrators. I traveled from Wisconsin (where I was living at the time) down to North Carolina, toured the campus, met with faculty/staff, and spent considerable time chatting with the head of the program who encouraged me to apply again the following year.

After my visit, I knew my intuition was correct. This was the school I would attend, even if I had to wait a while for admission.

Upon my return home I explored possible scenarios to pursue for the next year: continue with my current job, explore temporary employment, or make the move down to North Carolina near the graduate school and settle in while I waited to apply during the next round of admissions. As with most periods of uncertainty, this time was full of hesitation and second-guessing.

And then one day, much to my surprise, I received a letter from the school informing me that I was accepted into the program . . . that year! Apparently, after considering all the intention, interest, and seriousness I had expressed in the interviews, they had waived the mandatory test scores and accepted me to the program.

Fast forward to graduation. I finished the program with a flawless record. I also ended up forming a close friendship with the department head, whom I met on my original visit. He was a significant mentor during my education.

This story certainly involves initiative and effort, which was critical, but what was most enlightening for me was the intuition aspect. I could have pursued admission into plenty of other schools, many of which were easier to get into, but I didn't. Something almost instinctual directed me toward this particular school and this draw was the catalyst for all that followed.

I see intuition play a part in the lives of almost all of my coaching clients. Intuition is also involved in my consultations with corporations on workplace culture, leadership, EQ, and team effectiveness. Typically, coaches are there not just to give answers to questions, but also to help clients explore challenges, evaluate resources, and set goals. You might even say that coaches help clients unearth truths deep within themselves but perhaps out of their conscious awareness. In this way, they help clients access their own intuition.

I have worked with many team and organization leaders whose biggest challenge is committing to the solution that they had already been considering. I've also worked with teams in which most members share a certain hesitation about one member. They know something needs to be addressed but are unsure how to communicate it, and this uncertainty makes them nervous. Usually, it's an intuition that the team member in question is hindering the team.

It's a common misconception that because intuition defies explanation, others probably don't feel the same way. I've seen it time and again: someone has an intuition about another member of the group but is too nervous to speak up because they think they're the only one who feels that way. If and when they do speak up, what they often encounter is that their intuition was common among many group members all along, and that everyone else was just as nervous about saying something. What they dismissed as their own private thought turned out to be the elephant in the room.

The only solution is to speak up. Once teams get comfortable with calling out what they intuit, they can move past challenges and conflict rapidly. Admittedly, this is not easy. It takes lots of practice and a willingness to deal with what can be a steep learning curve. Once it becomes status quo among members, gains in performance and productivity ensue.

Similarly, I have worked with many leaders who have a sense that something needs to change, but aren't quite sure what it is and how to change it. They may have heard general complaints among employees or management. In some cases, these leaders may just have an intuition that something is off. Perhaps there is something about their leadership that just isn't working. Whatever it is, they don't know how to approach their organization about it. The challenge then becomes building in strategies for collecting feedback regularly as well as employing more effective communication practices. Learning how to let go of control or ego in order to truly hear the feedback also comes into play. Listening is an art and a science.

When I work with clients on interpersonal dynamics within the team or leadership, they usually speak up about their intuitions. We usually discuss things like transparency, communication, how to resolve conflict, or how to give feedback for example. I cannot think of a time when a leader or team member I've worked with followed their intuition and didn't find value from the decision. Not that intuition is correct 100 percent of the time, but following it always leads to some lesson or discussion. In short, there is always much to be gained.

Here are some helpful strategies to explore when considering your own intuition:

EVALUATE HOW THIS DECISION RELATES TO OLD PATTERNS

Does the decision you are leaning toward fit into a habit or pattern for you, or would you describe it as more of an instinct? If you are unsure if it is an old habit or not, consider making a list of similar decisions you have had to make and how you've approached them. Hopefully this evaluation will reveal a pattern. You can then choose to either stick to your regular game plan or break the pattern if it doesn't serve your success and development.

FEAR WRAPPED UP IN INTUITION

When you have a hunch regarding a certain decision, test to see if it is not actually fear in disguise. Fear, posing as intuition, can show up to prevent an action or decision that may be unfamiliar or uncomfortable. Just because something is uncomfortable doesn't mean it isn't valuable. This begs the question, "**How** *does one distinguish intuition from fear?*" It's one of life's biggest challenges, of course, and it requires a brutally honest and thorough assessment of your tendencies. The more you assess, the clearer the distinction will become. In your assessment, consider asking yourself the following questions:

- *Is the decision I'm leaning toward based on what I think is safest? If so, is this tendency toward safety truly helping me at this moment? (For example, if you feel an inner resistance to exploring a new relationship because you don't want to get hurt, ask yourself if this emotional self-preservation isn't undermining your desire to be in a fulfilling relationship.)*
- *Does your behavior go beyond misguided self-preservation? Is there any* **self-sabotage** *connected to this hunch? In other words, could my decision be based on any previous pattern of finding opportunities and then undercutting them in a variety of ways?*
- *Is my decision somehow connected to a previous trauma of some kind? For example, could a hunch about a new job not working out relate in any way to a childhood of constantly being called a failure?*

If these questions are too challenging to explore on your own, consider working with a therapist or coach to help you unpack your truth. For more information on addressing fear, see Chapter 13. For more information on how to find the right therapist or coach, see Part Two.

There is a real advantage and opportunity in checking the influence of fear or discomfort in your decision-making.

Just a reminder: we are rarely 100 percent certain of any decision, but that should not cripple us with indecision. Learning to trust our intuition includes accepting a certain degree of uncertainty. (More on this in chapter 19.)

WHAT IS THE IMPACT OF THIS DECISION IN 5 YEARS OR 20 YEARS

Weigh the consequences of your decisions. For instance, if this decision won't make that big of a difference in five years, then perhaps it's fine to move forward. On the other hand, combining intuition with some logic may be worth exploring if this decision will still impact you in twenty years. Of course, this question is hard to answer with certainty, and that's okay. The process of exploration may lead to insight. You may come to greater understanding of the potential longer-term repercussions of your decision. You can't predict the future, so get comfortable with the uncertainty.

IF I DON'T TRUST THIS INTUITION, WILL THE RESULT BE REGRET OR POTENTIAL FAILURE?

Remember, logic and reason are important, but so is taking risks. Change occurs at the edge of comfort. Ask yourself if the decision will likely produce fear or regret for not doing something different. A little fear isn't a bad thing.

Consider this quote by the famous comedienne, Lucille Ball:

*"I'd rather regret the things I've done
than regret the things I haven't done."*

HOW HAS MY INTUITION BEEN ACCURATE IN THE PAST AND WHERE HAS IT LED ME?

Looking at past gains and losses can be advantageous. You know the feeling you get when you look back at something and think, *"My gut told me to do _____. I wish I would have listened"*? This is what I'm referring to. Hindsight is 20/20, but what you actually do with this hindsight/insight and how you make shifts going forward is what counts. Don't just look back, shrug it off, and dismiss the learning. We're bound to make mistakes, but we're not cursed to keep making the *same* mistakes.

Making a list of the times intuition has led to positive results may help bolster self-confidence. Exploring what prevented you from following your gut in the first place is also valuable. Take the time, do the work, identify the patterns. This way you can make more appropriate decisions in the future.

CHAPTER 5 ACTIVITY

How has intuition worked for you? Start by tracking instances in which intuition comes into play. This activity offers you a chance to evaluate your decisions in those moments.

Look at the patterns that emerge in your behavior and consider if trusting your more intuitive self has worked out in the past. Recall times you trusted your intuition and times you didn't. After you have recounted a few memories, see if you notice how, on the whole, trusting your intuition has been more valuable or more detrimental? Remember, the important part is the evaluation. Examining your choices and the results allows you to determine what is driving them, intuition or fear. Sometimes we may think something is intuition, but in actuality it is fear holding the wheel. This evaluation allows you to uncover the patterns.

See the example for assistance:

EXAMPLE 1: TO PURCHASE A CAR AFTER GETTING A NEW JOB

- *Intuition: Told me to wait six months*
- *Decision: Purchased car right away*
- *Result: I was stressed out for six months due to uncertainty about the job and money I spent*

6

THE IMPORTANCE
OF GRATITUDE

H ere are three important
reasons for expressing gratitude.

1. Recognizing all you are thankful for helps to maintain perspective when feeling stressed.
2. Gratitude improves life socially, psychologically, and even physically.
3. Expressing gratitude creates positive chain reactions. It has an emotional effect on others and makes them more likely to express gratitude in turn.

Gratitude is tremendously important for many more reasons than those listed above. If you haven't yet experienced the power of gratitude, it is my hope that by the end of this chapter you'll be convinced.

As a quick disclaimer, though, when I use the phrase *"gratitude,"* I'm referring to both how it registers within one's self and how it is expressed to others through word and deed. One must not only *feel* grateful, but *express* gratitude to get the full benefit of what I will discuss at length in this chapter. The feeling of gratitude and the expression of it are linked. You may even say that they form a virtuous cycle, one reinforcing the other.

Expressing gratitude can intensify such feelings. Even if you don't feel as grateful as you think you ought to, expressing the gratitude that you believe is possible, ironically perhaps, sparks genuine feeling within.

In my work over the years, I have encountered a common misconception about gratitude. Some confuse it as a silver bullet that will magically change your life. Gratitude isn't about *"thinking happy thoughts to change your life."* Rather, it is being appreciative of one's circumstances, recognizing all that we have and acting accordingly. Identifying ways to be grateful may change how you think and feel over time, but identification without action may not produce the change you're seeking. It is the application of gratitude that moves the needle. You need to find the proper expressions of gratitude. There is opportunity to take action and express gratitude every day. Think of the coworker who pitched in extra time on your project; your spouse, who helps you in various ways throughout the week; or the barista who was extra friendly one morning. We all know how meaningful it is when our efforts are acknowledged. The important part about practicing gratitude is to express it with specificity and sincerity.

That said, you have lots to be grateful for. I promise.

If you are reading this book, you most likely have some disposable income. Let me put the term in perspective. According to the website, The Global Rich List, if you made $32,400 (USD) in 2016, you qualified as the top one percent of the global society, i.e. every human being on the planet.[18] Granted, this is in context of global wealth disparity, but you get the point. The unfortunate piece of this puzzle is that there are those who will never see $32,400 in a lifetime—the majority of the global population, in fact.

Curious what the top one percent looks like within U.S. borders? The numbers rise exponentially. According to Kiplinger, in recent years, it takes about $430,000 of adjusted gross income to reach the top one percent of U.S. income earners.[19]

Let me be clear about this. I don't bring up these numbers to show you that gratitude is exclusive to the haves and that misery is exclusive to the have-nots. Often, it is the exact opposite. I bring money to your attention because it is conveniently quantifiable. It is only one facet of your existence, but one on which you can gain some perspective. There are many other areas in our lives to be grateful for: relationships, family, work, health, mind, and all the many freedoms we have. Also, donuts.

THREE MORE REASONS WHY EXPRESSING GRATITUDE MAY BE BENEFICIAL TO YOU

1. According to Robert Emmons, a leading researcher on gratitude, there are several benefits to expressing gratitude on a regular basis, including a stronger immune system, higher levels of positive emotions, a more forgiving attitude, and fewer feelings of isolation.[20] In a study published by the *Journal of the Society for Psychotherapy Research*, it was found that routinely journaling about what one is grateful for had a positive impact on mental health as reported by participants.[21]

2. Expressing gratitude has an impact on your relationships. According to Dr. John Gottman, a leading expert in marital relationships, it is very important for a couple to maintain a ratio

of more positive interactions than negative for the marriage to be successful.[22] For example, if you can focus more on your gratitude for your partner instead of how they didn't take out the garbage (again), it's likely to bode well for your future together.

3. Gratitude has an impact on others around you. If you want to make a difference in how you interact with others, consider adding an element of gratitude. This shift in interaction style may have a significant impact on your relationships and the quality of your communication. Experiment with this. Consider all the qualities of individuals or situations that you appreciate when you come across them. This can happen at work, during or after challenging experiences, and with family, friends, and even people who you swear exist just to make you miserable. Assume that they have appeared in your life for a reason and that you get to choose what they are teaching you.

Consider asking yourself the following questions:

- *What am I willing to learn from this person/situation?*
- *What have I learned about myself through the time spent with this person/situation?*
- *What am I now able to do as a result of my interaction with this person/situation?*
- *On a more general level, what do I have access to on a daily basis that I take for granted?*
- *If I were forced to let go of three things that are most important to me, what would they be, how would the loss affect me, and, based on this realization, how can I offer more gratitude for them now, when I still have them?*

Sometimes gratitude isn't immediate. In times of true chaos, considering what you're grateful for may be the last thing on your mind. I know that during particularly challenging times in my life, it was always difficult to identify the gratitude amidst it all.

In my early thirties, I experienced one of the toughest experiences of my life. I went through a separation with a woman, who I was certain would be my lifelong partner. This break was so devastating that my view of my entire future shifted. I had to reassess my desires, my philosophies on life, and the direction I was heading. This experience was a game-changer. At the time, I had difficulty seeing beyond the pain, but like with most things, time offers perspective.

We had been living in a small town in western North Carolina. After the separation, I left the home we'd been sharing and moved back to where I grew up, in south east Wisconsin. I worked on my family's farm for six months while I tried to figure out what to do next.

Looking back, I think I had been assuming things would work out with this person in the future and that our issues would eventually resolve themselves. In less than six months, however, she was pregnant and engaged to someone else. It was another shock, which amplified the heartbreak and self-loathing. In retrospect, I think I had put more stock in our potential reconnection than I was willing to admit.

Finding gratitude at the time seemed like a total joke. As I was consumed with anger, resentment, and confusion, accessing gratitude felt near-impossible. There were a few things that pulled me through the experience: perspective, faith, work, and distraction. Even though my capacity for gratitude at the time was limited, it was my daily contemplation on all that I had that proved most significant in restoring peace of mind in the end.

The truth was, I had supportive friends and family in my life, a strong education, an extensive network to draw on for opportunity, my health, and all basic needs met. Even just being grateful for the most basic of things can be a daily dose of relief. When we whittle down all that we have to all that we really need, most of us are richer than we think. Gratitude helps us to focus on what is right in front of us.

Certainly during a time when we are immersed in pain, gratitude may be difficult to access. But when we are able to look back on things, it becomes easier and more comprehensive. If we allow it to, that is. Today, years after the breakup, I deeply appreciate all the lessons learned from this person and the experience. I believe I can say that without trivializing the pain of the experience, as it has taken a long time to arrive at this perspective. You could say we are always arriving.

I spent a long time with anger, regret, disbelief, heartache, and fear. But now I am able to see the silver lining in the process. I can now look back with appreciation and see how I was pushed toward greater motivation, life purpose, resiliency, and compassion. Through gratitude, insight, and choice, I was able to use the pain to fuel an important transformation.

Now, as time has passed, I see how the path I chose led to opportunity and connection. My move back to where I grew up led to a great work opportunity, which set me on course for exploring my current career and starting my own business. More than that, though, the experience compelled me to ask myself some important questions. I had the opportunity to evaluate what was meaningful to me: what kind of future I wanted, what kind of partner I wanted, and what professional and personal goals I sought to put in place.

Some of the toughest questions highlighted my own culpability in the decay of the relationship. I took a long, hard look at my own selfishness and lack of communication and realized that I hadn't acted with as much empathy as I had assumed. With a greater understanding of my faults, I was able to work on being a better partner in the future.

I will remain grateful to my ex-girlfriend for these lessons. But let's remember, I was only able to adopt this perspective after moving away from the mode of victim and into the mode of master (see Chapter 1).

Being patient with ourselves is important. Often, resolution just takes time. (We'll take a closer look at timing and pacing in Chapter 8.) I do believe practice speeds things up, though. Asking *"What am I grateful for?"* may be an easier or harder question to answer, depending on the day. However, just like everything else, with practice, it becomes easier. Intention leads to practice, which leads to habit, which eventually leads to sustainable change.

CHAPTER 6 ACTIVITY

Follow these steps to begin showing more gratitude. You'll have the opportunity to work through your own gratitude list and share your learning with others. Want to see how gratitude really works? Don't keep it a secret.

1. **Think of someone or something you are grateful for right now and why.**

2. **Express this gratitude by writing a small thank you message.** This message could be a handwritten letter, a text, or an email or it could be delivered over social media. If you share it over social media, tag your recipient and express how they have impacted you.

3. **Share your gratitude experiment on social media and explain why you are doing it.** You can even tag someone in a *"gratitude invitation"* to apply the same experiment. Your motivation for working on this skill may be unique to you. But your joy and gratitude will have a ripple effect, causing others to consider their own reasons to be grateful.

4. **Move through the day with ease.**

ACTION

"I fear not the man who has practiced 10,000 kicks once, but I fear the man who has practiced one kick 10,000 times."

—**Bruce Lee**

We all have habits, routines, predispositions, and behaviors that we engage in every day. Some of these are helpful, some are harmful. Taking the time to evaluate our actions is a crucial step in change creation. But understanding alone doesn't create sustainable shifts. It is application of our insight that moves us to new heights.

It is the application of knowledge and the action we take that create sustainable change.

I often find myself repeating a version of this statement. When meeting with individual coaching clients or consulting with organizations, the idea of translating knowledge to action always comes up.

Taking action is paramount. Creating shifts in our thinking is an excellent first step. Changing how we think can lead to significant change in our life. Only by applying our insight to creating new habits, however, do we truly integrate our new paradigm. When we practice what we understand, we bring that understanding to life.

In this section, we'll explore how to translate your new insight into practice.

KNOWING ISN'T ENOUGH

Happy Holidays!

I'm glad you're here. In the spirit of the time of year, I want to offer a gift and a challenge. This idea comes from Will Bowen of A Complaint Free World. The reason for this gift is that there continues to be more and more evidence for the value of how we connect our thoughts, statements, actions, and feelings to our overall experience of the world. This challenge offers the opportunity to consider the things we say, if only for three weeks. Basically, no complaining. One strategy in tackling this seemingly insurmountable task is practicing gratitude. We all have much to be thankful for. Okay, I'll start. In this card, you'll find a few reasons why I am grateful to have you in my life. I hope you find this gift intriguing and interesting enough to experiment with.

Love,
Michael

This was the beginning of a Christmas card I passed around to friends and family a few years ago. I wanted to show some gratitude and give my loved ones a chance to put some intention into action for the New Year. I discovered this idea through Will Bowen's Complaint Free® challenge.[23]

The basic idea is that you try to make it through a full three weeks without complaining. The No Complaining Challenge starts with putting on a rubber bracelet. Every time you complain, you switch the bracelet to the other wrist, and the count starts over. According to the website, with all the starting over, this experiment typically takes participants 4 to 10 months to complete.[24] It's a true challenge that requires real dedication, but it also offers a valuable exercise in improving our outlook.

We often hear updated research about how to change our mindset, be more grateful, be more positive, etc. While I am totally on board with new insights, I believe it's just as important to find useful applications of these insights (like the examples in this chapter). This translation helps raise the likelihood of success in any change process. Whenever we adopt a new way of thinking or feeling, we also need to incorporate into our lives the practical counterpart: a new way of doing, acting, or behaving.

With every bracelet I gave, I attached a personal note, which explained why I was thankful to have that person in my life. I believe that including an expression of gratitude as part of the overall gesture was important because it added a positive element to the process of eliminating a negative.

I recommend getting a bracelet, or even a few, from A Complaint Free World. The exercise is definitely easier and more fun in a group because others help to keep you accountable.

As I've mentioned, if you are reading this book, then you most likely have your basic needs met. I imagine you also have some people in your life who matter to you and to whom you matter. There is much to be grateful for. Expressing gratitude is one strategy in combating the pattern of complaining because it shifts the focus and demands positive action.

"I'M WORKING ON THAT"

I've known plenty of leaders who think they have it all figured out. This next story is dedicated to the leaders who continue to search for insight and act on it.

When Charlene and I started working together, she was stressed. She was having a tough time dealing with her co-workers' incompetence and outright mistakes. She spent *hours and hours* putting out fires. It was one mess after another, and she finally reached her limit. She confided that she was on the edge of burnout.

Charlene managed multiple teams of people at her large healthcare company. Many people in her department knew her and respected her outgoing attitude and fierce dedication. Even though there were a good handful of people intimidated by her high energy, she was well liked.

What set Charlene apart was her will to improve. She was an aggressive goal setter and a voracious learner. She read twelve books, all on strengthening her leadership, in three months. In our work together, she would clearly articulate what she was learning and the leadership principles that she needed to focus on implementing: asking better questions, communicating with compassion, eliciting feedback, and setting clear expectations and boundaries with employees.

The challenge Charlene faced was managing stress. People stressed her out. She tried to hide her frustration, but wasn't always successful. She assumed that by applying her insights and the wisdom she'd absorbed through her study, she would be able to resolve her stress and become a better leader.

When asked to describe the exact applications she was experimenting with, however, she would brush it to the side with a *"Well, I'm working on that."* When challenged, she would struggle with any specifics. In other words, she had the *what*, but was missing the *how*.

Therefore, our work together mainly consisted of looking for opportunities to put her insights into motion, to find ways to practice them. For instance, we explored how she could conduct meetings in a way that would emphasize leadership principles. She worked on establishing clear expectation, improving structure, clarifying calls to action, and communicating deadlines. She would also practice communicating differently with co-workers and employees at these meetings. She practiced modulating her tone of voice, taking a breath to pace herself, and generally communicating in a calm and more curious manner.

She also practiced connecting with her co-workers by asking more questions and requesting specific feedback. By doing so, she was able to better understand the root of problems, not just symptoms. This may sound like a simple task, but it took serious diligence and accountability.

Through these specific applications, Charlene reduced her stress, increased productivity in her teams, and ultimately resolved much of the conflict and drama in her workplace. She also experienced a greater sense of control, not only in the office, but also at home. She was finally able to translate the insights she had long held into clear behaviors, and through this, effected sustainable change.

~

THE TABLECLOTH

When I was a senior in high school, my stepmother, Colleen, died of cancer. She was a wonderful, kind, fun, and energetic person whom I will always remember fondly. This story isn't about me or her, though. It's about my dad and his process of moving through change and grief.

She passed on February 6 after a few days of hospice at home. Due to everything going on in her final months, we hadn't gotten around to putting away all the holiday decorations. One of these was a bright red, gold-embroidered Christmas table-cloth covering the dining room table. As time passed, my dad put away the decorations and started to organize and donate his wife's belongings, as you'd imagine.

The table cloth remained. Months went by, but he couldn't bring himself to put it away. It reminded him of her. It created a sense of connection. Replacing the table cloth would be one more way of letting her go. Though he had said goodbye in other ways, he had a tough time with this one.

This is often where we get stuck. We know what we need to do in the midst of change or a life transition, but knowing isn't enough. We must translate that knowledge into action.

When I asked my dad how he managed to finally remove the table cloth, I was expecting a dramatic moment. But he just laughed and said that it simply needed a cleaning. When he finally took off the cloth, he made a discovery. He had forgotten about the beautiful, stained cherry wood tabletop, covered up all those long months.

When we find the courage to act, there are often positive surprises on the other side. By their very nature, these surprises cannot be predicted. You need to have faith that you'll find them when you get there. As such, trials like these require three of the principles outlined in this book: Action, Guts, and Spirit.

The act of removing the table cloth, which my dad kept postponing, took on new meaning for him when he finally did it. By acting on what he knew he had to do, he was finally able to make sustainable change. He has replaced the tablecloth with placemats as a reminder that holding on to the pain wasn't serving him. He does take out the tablecloth every holiday season, however, to celebrate Colleen's memory.

CHAPTER 7 ACTIVITY

Which of your insights do you still need to turn into action?

The next time you realize that certain knowledge you have about a particular area of your development has yet to be applied, do something about it. You can use the three stories in this chapter as inspiration. Each of the activities below correlate with each of the stories.

1. Take note when you are about to complain, and see how you can shift your would-be complaint into a statement of gratitude. Keep track! Write down your *"reactive"* complaint and then write down the kind of grateful *"response"* that you could substitute. Also, begin to log times you almost complained but were able to stop yourself.

2. Have you read a book or attended a course or conference recently? If so, my guess is that there is an opportunity to implement the new information you have acquired. Don't buy that next book, conference ticket, or webinar until you've implemented what you learned from the last. Do a trial run by instituting one lesson or principle for one month. Write down how exactly you are enacting the specific behaviors connected to the learning that you have gained. This ensures that you will have a specific, concrete answer to the all-important question, HOW am I applying what I have learned?

3. Have you been postponing the all-important step of putting insight into practice? Perhaps you know what you need to do, but haven't been able to overcome your natural resis-

tance. Now is the time to let go of that resistance. Answer the following questions and then take action!

- *How might things be different once you take action?*
- *What do you risk by taking action?*
- *What support can you get that will help you take action and follow through?*

For free tips, tools and strategies to take action toward positive change, even when change is hard, visit: www.arcintegrated.com/changes

8

THE PACE OF CHANGE

"It's not a sprint, it's a marathon" is a phrase often used to help people avoid expending undue energy at the beginning of a new endeavor. But what does this mean in regard to adapting to change and inviting it into our lives? To maintain long-term success with change, you need to practice regularly and diligently over long periods of time. You can't implement everything you learn all at once. But, as you grow and develop, you can achieve more by using each goal you reach as a stepping stone to the next.

One strategy proven to be effective in implementing and maintaining change is the concept of a daily practice. I've seen the implementation of a daily practice help a wide variety of clients make a wide variety of changes. (More about the daily practice in chapter 11.)

Keeping to a daily routine is also a common trait among some of the most successful people in the world. By the way, when I refer to daily practice, I'm not referring to watching the latest show on Netflix night after night. I'm referring to a practice of self-cultivation that occurs every day.

Regardless of what field they are in, be it finance, athletics, philosophy, art, etc., society's most accomplished individuals find that a daily routine establishes stability and order. Virgin founder and philanthropist Richard Branson describes his daily morning routine as involving exercise, breakfast, and mindful family time before he starts work. Also, according to *Business Insider*, he always carries a notebook.[25] Journaling is another practice that is often found in daily routines.

Tony Robbins (the famous seminar leader, author, speaker, philanthropist, and coach) has kept up a morning routine that consists of meditation, exercise, and a cold water plunge. Tim Ferriss, the multi-award winning author and dissector of *"all things optimized"* has a morning routine as well. He identifies meditation, tea drinking, journaling, a light breakfast, and exercise all as key parts of his morning.

These are just a few examples of peak performers and their recipes for success.

The term *"success"* is relative, though, often inappropriately defining someone who has a great deal of money. As you may have gathered thus far, true success comes from self-knowledge: knowing exactly who you are—your blind spots, your strengths, habits, etc. Through this self-knowledge we can authentically define what success looks like for us and what prevents us from achieving it. Now, that might mean that for you success is still a pile of money, but not necessarily. (See Chapter 15 for more about success.)

Through development and disciplined practice of my daily routine, I have learned a lot about my strengths and weaknesses, including what draws me back to old, unfulfilling habits. This is another value of the routine: it exposes parts of ourselves that we may not have been aware of. A therapist once told me something about habit that has stuck with me through the years. We were discussing the challenge of steering clear of old, unhealthy habits. She said:

"In the most intense times of stress, we regress to our least sophisticated coping methods."

The truth of this statement continues to resonate in my observations of myself and others. When working with any client, from business executives building leadership skills to coaching clients working through a career change, the element of daily practice always comes up. Practicing new skills daily helps us reduce the likelihood of defaulting to our less effective, but more familiar coping methods. When we fail to concentrate on the skills, habits, and perspectives necessary to create sustainable change, we are likely to fall back into our ruts. We resort to drinking too much alcohol, spending too much time on the couch, eating foods that don't nourish our bodies, using anger to express ourselves too often, or defaulting to other patterns that do not serve us well. In the chapters that follow, you'll find details on how to successfully incorporate daily practice.

Instilling permanent change in behavior or establishing a new pattern takes time. To help you remember this very important point, remember to pace yourself.

P.A.C.E.

Patience

Acceptance

Control

Empathy

The terms: patience, acceptance, control, and empathy, are all critical to sustaining any change. Even outside of creating change, applying these terms will help you through many of life's challenges. As they relate specifically to change, let me explain:

Patience – Since we know change takes time, patience is of utmost importance. Often, changes are not successful because we don't practice long enough. We don't wait until the new pattern sets in as habit. Being patient in your process as you create a new way of living can strengthen resolve to continue. Let go of the pressure to change immediately. Learn to enjoy the process. A daily practice gives you something to look forward to, to count on, and to help you build patience.

Acceptance – During a lifestyle shift, some days will be great, others not so much. Accept these vacillations as a normal part of the process like the ebb and flow of the tide. During your practice of implementing a change, you may encounter more difficulty than you did yesterday. That does not mean you failed. Or maybe it's simply a matter of perspective. If you did fail, it's not a big deal; you only failed for a day! It's only temporary. Failure is only a problem if you allow it to create a negative space in your head, if you feed it with fixation and let it reproduce. It only becomes a barrier when you wallow, give up, or reject the possibility that you can pick it back up tomorrow and start anew. Challenges are likely to present themselves when you are in the midst of change. It is important to accept what may be out of your control and to move on as soon as you can.

Control – When you're on the path toward change, it is critical to consider the idea of control—knowing what is within your control and what isn't. Intimately connected to the idea of acceptance, control relates more to your perception of a situation than to the actual event itself. When faced with a challenge, we still have the ability to control our interpretation of the situation. As I detailed earlier, we have the choice to be victims or masters of our challenges. So, remember, optimize your strengths, investigate your complaints before you give them voice (see Chapter 7), and allow your failures to be teachers—think *gratitude.*

In all change processes, there will be things you cannot control. Identify what is in your control and what isn't. You can then apply acceptance to those elements that you can't control. If this sounds like the Serenity Prayer, it's no coincidence. Regardless of your religious faith or lack thereof, the Serenity Prayer is another great resource to reference when moving through a challenging change process. (For more on this, see Section 7 – Spirit.)

Empathy – Having empathy for yourself through the process of change is crucial. So, what does self-empathy mean? It means staying connected to yourself in the process, allowing yourself to make mistakes along the way, and knowing that it is okay. Allowing yourself to make mistakes and not giving up is a recipe for lasting change. For example, there will be times when you plan to implement a change or practice a new behavior and you experience a setback due to old patterns. It's natural to have setbacks, just don't let those setbacks translate into a quitting mindset.

Two additional roadblocks to empathy are guilt and shame. Being mindful of the hiccups along the way toward change is great, as long as it's productive. You know what isn't productive? Talking to yourself like you're a bully on a middle school playground. This is where shame can rear its ugly head. Dr. Brené Brown, the brilliant professor and sociologist, talks about shame as a focus on self and guilt as a focus on behavior. The difference between *"I am bad"* (shame) and *"I did something bad"* (guilt.)[26]

If you're like a lot of people, you have the nasty habit of scolding yourself for doing something wrong. Get over it! You're human. Shaming yourself only leads to stagnation in your otherwise positive process. Be kind to yourself. Be forgiving. Reserving some of your compassion for yourself increases the likelihood of pushing successfully through setbacks and ultimately helps you reach your goals. Building self-empathy is also a component of emotional intelligence, as we explored in Chapter 4.

So, next time you are facing a change or working toward a goal, consider how you can PACE yourself.

CHAPTER 8 ACTIVITY

There are two parts to this activity. First, explore a goal you are working toward, something you are trying to change. Write down this goal in detail.

Second, write out how you can apply the concepts of PACE to reaching your goal. For each letter of the acronym, assign a specific action to take. Remember, successful change is about more than mere understanding; it is about translating understanding into action.

Example: Trying to meditate every day

- **Patience:** *There will inevitably be days on which I fail to meditate, but I will almost always be able to reach my goal of meditating five times per week.*

- **Acceptance:** *I may not be able to meditate every morning but I have been able to meditate at some point during the day.*

- **Control:** *There have been some emergencies that have required my attention and have impacted the pursuit of my goal. Some things are out of my control. But I still have the power to re-prioritize the items on my day's agenda and perhaps to make sacrifices to reach my goal.*

- **Empathy:** *I can accept that it may take time to create a new habit and that if my pace is slower than expected, it doesn't mean I am a failure.*

9

THE BEST WAY TO IMPROVE PRODUCTIVITY

A close friend of mine used to work for a major airline. She was in charge of baggage and cargo handling and all the processes involved. One item proved particularly tricky to ship, horse sperm. That's right, you read that correctly. Funny enough, its handling is a delicate process, given the enormous financial stakes in the racehorse industry and the sensitivity of the substance. As I understand it, there was much debate about the fastest and most efficient way to transport the *"precious"* cargo. Even though there was an official procedure, the process also allowed for some independence. An individual's unique approach to any task is significant, and this is where disagreements ensue. Each cargo worker had a different notion about how to expedite the process. Now you might be asking, what does shipping horse sperm have to do with productivity. The point here is the individuality of the process, which is the heart of this chapter.

It's always advantageous to evaluate the fit between someone's particular strengths and their work. Companies use this process to improve productivity. One way to do this is to assess the individual's personality and examine the characteristics needed in the position they are in and compare the two. It makes sense that when we align an employee's values, motivations, and personality with a job that benefits from these characteristics, everyone wins. The employee is happier because the work comes more naturally and the company sees more productivity.

You know this intuitively. Think of a time when you've felt lost in a task. You looked up and hours had gone by. This lost sense of time, sometimes referred to as *"flow,"* often derives from a match between skill, interest, and task requirement. We are productive when we are engaged. Conversely, the more of a disconnect there is between skills/values and the task at hand, the harder it will be to enhance productivity.

I once worked with a manufacturing company looking for a new salesperson. The company thought the position required a particular profile. Through our discussion about the position and the person in mind, we determined which values, motivators, and communication style the position demanded. When we finished our work together, the company also had a more robust understanding of how to motivate the person in the position. They could see a few potential challenges with the candidate, strengths the candidate had, and how the company could optimize those strengths.

There are certainly other factors that will affect productivity. There are also an endless amount of resources available to us that promise to improve it. While I have not found a definitive *"best way"* to improve productivity in my search, I do believe that some ways are better than others. Optimizing productivity is always dependent on the individual. You will find the way best for you by experimenting with a wide range of techniques and practices.

A good first step toward increased productivity may require eliminating a negative instead of adding a positive. Find ways to address your tendencies toward laziness, distraction, or inefficiency. To repeat, the most effective way to improve productivity will be the one that is most closely connected to you. That new life hack you read or heard about might be useful to you, but only if it taps into something personal. As you frantically search Google for the latest *"best"* tips, consider what might be the best fit for you. Yes, this may take some action and experimentation to uncover what works best.

Self-exploration calls for testing out different strategies and seeing what sticks. See what works for you. When looking to identify which kinds of practices to experiment with, a good place to start might be online lists such as a post on one of London's leading tech blogs titled *"Boosting Personal Productivity in Real Life,"* which offers helpful tips and strategies.[27]

Experimentation followed by practice is where the rubber hits the road. Using strategies that are most closely connected to you will yield the best results.

There are certainly some exercises and strategies that are more about self-exploration than others. Below I have included a concise list of strategies that may help to improve productivity. More importantly, though, this list offers the opportunity to explore what's holding you back. Without exploration of who we are at our core (values, beliefs, habits, reactions, etc.), our ability to improve our own productivity will be limited.

PERSONAL DEVELOPMENT AND PRODUCTIVITY

BATCH YOUR WORK

There is a common misconception among us worker bees. When we feel overwhelmed with all there is to do it is usually because we are having a tough time prioritizing. And so, foolishly, we try to tackle everything at once. Sometimes this isn't even our intention but our to-do lists, work pressures, and personal obligations often put us in a frenzy to finish everything all at the same time. When we tackle things systematically, however, we are often more productive. Batching our work is essentially designating a specific amount of time for a particular task. For instance, limiting your email to one hour a day or your sales calls to Thursday mornings. It doesn't matter what the task is, the idea is that you set specific times for specific tasks. Batching your work is a great experiment if you haven't attempted it before. It not only improves productivity but also keeps us prioritized and even reduces stress. For example, try responding to emails only two times per day, at two specific times (9:00 a.m. and 3:00 p.m., for example) for a two-week period. For the rest of the day, let it go. You might be surprised how this boosts efficiency and quells the internal urge to *"always be available."*

CREATE A DAILY PRACTICE

Sound familiar? Yes, I've already brought this up. I bring it up again as a reminder of how important it is! Among successful people, one thing is consistent: they maintain some sort of regular practice that helps them focus.[28] Having a daily practice helps to boost mindfulness, discipline, and stability—all things that improve productivity.

PRACTICE DISCIPLINE EVERYDAY

Similar to the daily practice, practicing discipline can help you build routine and productivity in many areas in your life. Discipline can be practiced in several ways: through fitness, healthy eating, work duties, behavior in relationships, self-reflection, etc. The practice of discipline may be just as important in itself as the goal related to it. (More about discipline in Chapter 14.)

GET UP AND MOVE

You may have heard the commentary about sitting being the new smoking.[29] There is substantial research to back up the idea that a sedentary lifestyle poses significant risks to health, well-being, and productivity. Exploring ways that can help you enjoy regular daily movement will make these little light-exercise breaks easier to commit to and more likely to stick. For instance, you may need more motivation to hit the gym than the prospect of running on a treadmill. Activities such as racquetball, kickboxing, yoga, spin class, pilates, trail running, team sports or even ping pong, may get your blood moving and also hold your interest.

Again, this is about personally exploring what works for you. You don't have time in your super-busy, really important day? Consider getting a standing desk. Or, if you're really a go-getter, a treadmill desk. Yes, they really do exist. Some people find them to be major productivity enhancers.

EXPLORE YOUR PASSIONS AND PURPOSE

We are often more productive if we are doing something we really care about. Yes, I understand that our passions only extend so far, that bills need to be paid, meetings need to be attended, conflicts need to be resolved, and toilets need to be cleaned. But remember, these things are connected. Understanding where our passions lie and what we find meaning in can often help to motivate us through some of the more challenging periods of our daily lives. If you aren't sure, that's okay, start experimenting. Start with a few questions in this chapter's activity.

TIME ANALYSIS

Every time I have done this activity or worked with a client who was doing it, I have seen positive results. The exercise is simple. Bear with me, though, as it might sound a bit daunting at first. The basic idea is to track every 15-minute increment of your day to assess how you really spend your time. This doesn't mean you need to be writing down reflections every 15 minutes, but at the end of the day you should be able to account for every 15 minutes. An easy way to do this is by creating a simple spreadsheet and filling in cells that designate each 15-minute increment of the day. At the end of the day, all your time needs to be accounted for, from the time you wake in the morning to the time you drift off to sleep at night. Now this requires some serious honesty, so don't cheat. If it turns out you spent three and a half hours watching Game of Thrones on a Monday, then this is the reality. After doing this analysis for a couple of weeks, you'll learn lots about how you're spending your time and how to improve your productivity.

TAKE A VACATION

This may seem counterintuitive since on the surface taking a vacation does not seem like the most productive of activities. But letting go of some of life's demands and distancing yourself from the hustle, even if only for a few days, can sharpen your vision and help you identify what is truly important when you return. After some mental rest, you may also experience a boost of energy.

CHAPTER 9 ACTIVITY

The first step in boosting productivity is taking an assessment of what has worked in the past and exploring what's available to you. When you evaluate, be creative. Don't just consider the activities themselves, but all aspects pertaining to the activities. Use your responses to get you started on your way to increased productivity.

1) List five activities so engaging that you lose track of time when you do them. After you have completed your list, what themes emerge? Based on the themes, can you draw any conclusions that will keep you productive?

2) On days you are particularly productive, what circumstances stand out? For example, did you modify your activities, eating, or sleep routines, location, etc.? Write down everything that is unique about those super-productive days.

3) Think of five people you know who are highly productive. Interview these people about their routines, practices, and daily habits. See if you can identify patterns or themes that stand out about these people.

4) Based on what you have learned in this chapter, choose three actions and commit to them.

NOURISHMENT

*"There is more wisdom in your body
than in your deepest philosophy."*

—Friedrich Nietzsche

What we put in our bodies, how we choose to move, and the amount of rest we allow ourselves all influence our ability to thrive. All the aspects of self-nourishment have implications on how we function. Our nourishment impacts our relationships, reactivity, ability to create the change we seek, and stress management.

A simple change in diet, level of activity, or amount of sleep can create opportunity or wreak havoc on our ability to manage the pressures of daily life. Your ability to manage stress in your professional and personal life will impact your ability to create change. In this section, we'll explore the connection between the mind and the body and strategies on how to optimize this connection for your success.

10

THE MIND-BODY CONNECTION

I look back on my experience in graduate school fondly. One of the tracks of study I took while there was called Body Centered Therapy. It is described as *"A program designed to prepare students with an understanding of creative and expressive processes within the context of the mind-body connection."* The study of mind and body connectivity continues to evolve. Since it includes so many points of discussion, consider this chapter a brief introduction. I include this chapter because I have seen striking instances of clients utilizing the mind-body connection to create the change they want.

Making the mind-body connection is not only valuable, it is necessary. I once worked with a young client who could only really communicate well when he was in motion. For the purposes of this story, let's call him *"Ryan."* In his childhood, he had bounced from the care of various family members to foster homes to group homes.

In my career, I have worked with a number of group homes in a variety of ways, from managing teams of caseworkers and therapists to providing case support and therapy to clients. Primarily, I was there to help clients manage their behavior by reducing stress and building communication skills. Some of the stories I heard from the clients at these homes were truly heartbreaking. The recurring themes of violence, neglect, and abandonment defy description. But what was even more astonishing was the resilience of these kids. It was another great lesson, reminding me that people are capable of coming back from just about anything.

Ryan did not trust me at first. Considering the traumatic circumstances of his life, I expected no less. When Ryan and I met, I noticed that he would share and engage in conversation the most when we were walking around or playing basketball. So, when we met, I made sure that we were always moving. For reasons I'll explore in this chapter, the connection between the body and the mind is intricate and runs deep. For Ryan, though, it was simple: movement was safety and comfort. By tapping into what his body needed, he was able to feel safe enough to share some of his story. Even if this truth was not in his conscious awareness, it's what worked for him. While chatting on the move, Ryan and I were able to make some progress in navigating the challenges that he dealt with. He was able to compose himself in our time together so that he could begin to understand himself and communicate his needs. This is just one of many examples of clients who have drawn value from how the body and mind are connected.

There are many connections between an individual's physical experience (the body) and one's emotional well-being (the mind). For example, the 2015 article in *The Guardian*, *"Is Depression a Kind of Allergic Reaction?"* by Caroline Williams, makes the case that there may be a physical component related to the onset of depression.[30] This is not a new finding, however. Research has been connecting physical experiences with mental health issues for years. For example, the National Institute of Mental Health reviews published conclusions relating diabetes to depression.[31] Often, depression or anxiety results in physical symptoms. A descriptive map of physical experiences brought on by depression was published by *Healthline* in the 2017 article, *"The Effects of Depression in Your Body."*[32] For instance, we know anxiety and depression can bring on physical symptoms such as stomach ache, sweating, and/or headache.

Western practice tends to separate treatment of the body from treatment of the mind, but the notion of treating both together is gaining traction. The more we understand about the connection between experience, thought, behavior, and emotion, the more use practitioners make of a mind-body paradigm. Take depression, for example. Depression is a condition that impacts how we feel, think, and act (all involving the mind). Emotions such as sadness or worthlessness, both found in depression, can bring on real physical symptoms such as pain or nausea. And it goes both ways. There is also evidence to show that chronic illness contributes to depression.[33]

In regard to direct causes of mental health issues, there are a whole host of theories, which is to say it's a very complicated issue. Regardless of the cause, an overwhelming number of people respond well to lifestyle changes such as increased exercise, meditation, better sleep, and improved nutrition. Such positive responses strengthen the argument that to improve mental health one must address the connection between body and mind. And in this respect, I'm not just referring to clinical conditions, but also to the everyday challenges we all face with stress, overwhelm, sadness, frustration, defeatism, etc.

So, what do you do with all this information about the mind-body connection? You certainly don't need to be struggling with mental health challenges to see the benefits of adopting a more holistic approach to your life. A broader awareness leads to positive outcomes regardless of what kinds of challenges you may be facing.

Think about how to actively incorporate this new awareness into your daily life. You can change your perspective by changing how you respond to everyday situations. Try this: the next time you are faced with a stressful experience, stop and consider the impact on your body. Tense shoulders? Stooped posture? Stomach ache? Consider journaling about this experience.

For example, when feeling irritated by your roommate who keeps putting empty cartons of milk back in the fridge, consider your physical response. When the impatient driver behind you slams on the horn as soon as the light turns green or, on the other hand, when you receive an unexpected compliment from a stranger, take note of how your body feels. Whether positive or negative, your body undergoes an experience. Begin to track what you notice. Developing this mind-body awareness yields countless benefits. Here's a significant one: it helps to prevent harmful *reactions* and to facilitate healthy *responses*. (See The Four R's in Chapter 1.)

When you challenge old patterns of thinking about how your mind and body can work in unison instead of one struggling against the other, you begin to internalize and incorporate this new belief into your everyday habits. Soon, you will notice you don't have to remind yourself to think differently. Considering new or challenging situations from a mind-body perspective gives you the freedom to choose what is best for you without stressing either system.

MIND-BODY INTUITION

In Chapter 5, we explored how to cultivate intuition. Often, your body gives you clues about which decisions to make or hunches regarding which direction to take. You just need to learn to listen. Creating disciplined practices will help you develop this sensitivity.

I have consistently witnessed positive results when individuals and organizations apply a holistic mind-body approach to creating change. It should not be surprising that long-lasting change is achieved by addressing multiple components of the human experience simultaneously.

I am not alone in this belief. According to a 2009 article in *The Journal of Palliative Medicine*, a multimodal treatment approach, including mindfulness, meditation, yoga movement, and breathing exercises helped to reduce anxiety and depression in cancer patients.[34] Furthermore, in 2011 the *Canadian Journal of Counselling and Psychotherapy* published a study that highlighted the efficacy of using yoga as a complementary treatment to psychotherapy in treating people with depression and anxiety.[35] In 2013, the journal *Stress and Health*, referenced a study that found that a mind-body approach was effective in reducing stress in elementary school teachers.[36] These are just a few examples of how a mind-body approach can serve as an effective treatment for individuals and systems.

Acquiring information about lifestyle changes is a great place to start, but mere knowledge doesn't create change. Now that you have some new insight, it's time to put these ideas into action!

CHAPTER 10 ACTIVITY

Have you found any mind-body practices to be effective in your life? Whether you have or haven't, now is the time to experiment. Below you'll find opportunities to build a mind-body approach into the change process. Follow the instructions and take action!

Mind Your Body – There is extensive research to support the idea that lifestyle choices have a serious impact on our bodies and minds. When considering how to take care of your body, the basic tenets remain the same: eat whole foods, exercise regularly, and get plenty of sleep. Someone experiencing serious stress in his or her life may find these lifestyle changes more difficult to institute. Keep in mind, however, that these principles often reduces stress, which is always a welcome reprieve.

There are many resources out there so that you can continue to educate yourself on the mind-body connection. For more information on nutrition, wellness, the importance of sleep, as well as many other mind-body related insights, I recommend the following podcasts:

The Model Health Show.[37]

The Tim Ferriss Show.[38]

The Aubrey Marcus Podcast.[39]

Action Steps – Put a checkmark next to the action step that you'll do immediately. Come back within a month's time and complete the list. Consider doing a habit a week.

a. Listen to at least one episode of the following shows:

The Model Health Show _____

The Tim Ferriss Show _____

The Aubrey Marcus Podcast _____

b. Eat one meal per day that is only made up of whole foods _____

c. Commit to getting seven to nine hours of sleep, three times this week _____

d. Commit to rigorous exercise, at least, three times this week (yes, you have to sweat) _____

11

THE IMPORTANCE
OF SELF-CARE

In our world of busy schedules, high expectations, constant distractions, and technology-based information bombardment, self-care is not often enough a priority. So that we're all on the same page, let's define self-care. It consists of practices that help us to maintain or improve our emotional, physical, and mental well-being. Or, as a colleague of mine Dr. Agnes Wainman points out in an article on the website, *Psych Central*, self-care is *"something that refuels us, rather than takes from us."*[40] Self-care nurtures us. It helps us function at our highest levels. Common self-care practices include exercise, reading, journaling, meditation, communing with nature, and travel. But the list is endless because these practices reflect our own uniqueness.

We are constantly building on our understanding of the biology and neuroscience behind the factors in our overall sense of contentment, such as behavior, emotions, productivity, focus, and energy levels. Research shows that self-care not only affects the performance of individuals, but also that of organizations.[41]

Often stress leads to conflict. When we are stressed, our patience runs thin. When we run into interpersonal conflicts—with loved ones, co-workers, or strangers—our ability to respond appropriately is compromised. The solution to this conflict may be to take more time to care for ourselves.

This is not surprising news. When we feel better, can think more clearly, and are less stressed, we are more effective. So, regardless of what job you hold and what industry you work in, consider making your own care a priority.

Personally, the better I feel, the better I am at my work and in my relationships. Since I initiated a more regimented self-care routine, I have sharpened my focus, increased my productivity, and cultivated a calmer demeanor. Here's a little story about self-care:

In March of 2015, I slipped and fell from the top of a 75-foot waterfall. It was barely springtime in the Tennessee hills, and after months of freeze, the falls were starting to trickle once more. As I was trying to take a picture, the stump I was clutching on to for safety snapped. Caught off-balance, I slipped on some ice and went over the falls head first. I managed to invert myself and grab branches and rocks on the way down so that my free fall was reduced to about 30 feet before I landed in 18 inches of water on the rock bottom. I am very thankful for the years of martial arts training in which I learned to relax and focus during times of stress. I believe it was this, as well as exhaling on impact, that reduced physical injury.

I never lost consciousness, but I must have gone into shock. I recall dragging myself out of the shallow pool of water and doing a body-check for broken bones. Soaking wet, I worried that if I didn't get up and move, I'd soon get hypothermia.

My hiking companions ran down to where I had fallen and were shocked to find me in one piece. I couldn't have hiked the three miles out of the woods without them. I hung on to one guy, sometimes two. My body was in shock from the pain, which intensified along the way. My ankles swelled to twice the size, but thanks to good friends and good boots, I was able to make it back. Part of the consolation of that day was having witnesses because when I told the doctors about the fall, they didn't believe me.

After a series of x-rays, it was determined that I didn't break any bones. A miracle. I had plenty of rehabilitation work to do on my ankles and knees, but over time, I healed well. Just remember, sometimes getting the perfect picture isn't worth it.

Please take note here, the experience of the fall isn't the important part. It is the follow-up experience that I think offers the most value. I had a strong emotional reaction to the accident: feelings of gratitude, curiosity, wonder, fear etc. I kept coming back to the idea of *intentional living*, how deliberate I was with my time every day. When it comes to self-care, we need to be deliberate. We need to implement a sustainable practice, which requires just that: practice. My brush with death made me ask, *"How intentional are my moments, my days, my weeks, and my general direction in life?"* So, I created a self-care experiment, which I'll describe in detail momentarily. The experiment was originally supposed to last for 100 days, but it has gone on consistently since I began.

At the time of the accident I had lots of good things going on, and I was busy. But I wasn't as intentional or purposeful as I would have liked, so I decided to make a change. I learned there is a clear difference between being busy and actually being productive.

My experiment was informed by my study of daily practices during and after graduate school, my martial arts practice, and inspirational stories I had heard along the way about successful people and the routines, both physical and mental, that many incorporate.

So, why 100 days? It seemed like a nice round number and also more than enough time to form a new habit, which was my goal. Having a daily practice was not new for me, but I hadn't had any quite like this one, which was regimented and covered different focal points.

The order has had some variation, but for the most part this is how it goes:

- *I wake up, brush my teeth, splash some water on my face, and put in my contacts.*
- *I do 10 minutes of seated meditation. The meditation I do is mostly focused on relaxation and how I'm breathing. Sometimes I'll use a meditation device called MUSE, or the app, Calm. I meditate first because I've noticed that when I do so I'm better at recalling my dreams, which often offer nuggets of inspiration or learning.*
- *I do a short body warm-up, stretching and moving, and then a Tai Chi form that I have been practicing for the last 10 years or so. I'm at the point now that I can do this form with the familiarity and understanding that only comes with time, and yet I also still feel like a beginner. Any activity that keeps you both enthusiastic and humble is worth incorporating into your self-care routine.*
- *I then start a qigong routine. Qigong is another kind of meditation, which consists of held postures and slow, repetitive movements combined with breath and awareness.*

- *I then do 10-15 minutes of more intense movement, which gets my blood flowing even more. This exercise period is often longer, depending on my schedule. Usually, this portion of my routine consists of some combination of martial arts, push-ups, pull ups, sit ups, weight training, and stretching.*
- *To wrap up the routine, I write in a journal. My daily entry usually has three parts:*
  » *I write about whatever mood I wake up in or what's on my mind.*
  » *I write about the dreams I remember and what kind of meaning I can draw from them.*
  » *Most importantly, I write about my intention for the day and my gratitude. Sometimes, I write down intentions for longer-term goals, as they relate to what is happening in my life. I find that writing about gratitude is a helpful tool to stay present and focused. It also offers perspective, allowing us to compare all that we want to all that we already have. (See Chapter 6 for more on the power of gratitude.)*

Since I started this routine, I have felt better physically and have been more productive. I don't believe these positive changes are due to random coincidence. Creating clear daily goals and intentions leads to favorable outcomes. With such a routine in place, I spend my time in a more focused way, and that has helped me clarify the direction of my business and make headway on personal goals. With the clarity of mind and body that the routine cultivates, I tend to be more organized in my business, resulting in swifter and clearer progress.

On the best days, I am able to do the whole routine, but like everyone else, I encounter obligations and pressures that influence my decisions. On days I don't complete all of my routine,

I pick and choose the parts that hold the most significance for me. Each of our routines, like each of our stories, is unique. As mentioned in Chapter 8, a daily regimen is common among high performers across many disciplines. I have found that combining practices I enjoy with ones that are more of a struggle keeps me challenged and motivated, especially in the morning.

As of spring 2019, I will have maintained this routine for four consecutive years and plan to continue. What was once conceived of as a 100-day experiment has turned into many hundreds, thankfully. You'll find that as the regimen becomes a cornerstone of your day, the will to do it evolves into desire. If you are truly committed to exploring daily routine I highly recommend the book, *Own the Day, Own your Life*, by Aubrey Marcus. In it, Marcus takes a deep dive into the various aspects of a daily routine and covers a whole host of self-care practices.[42]

Experiment for yourself, and see what you find when you start making yourself a priority!

WAYS TO TAKE TIME FOR YOURSELF

Physical: Lift weights, run, walk, snowboard/ski, surf, take a class (spinning, CrossFit, yoga, martial arts, Zumba, etc.), hike, play golf, bike, have sex, etc.[43]

Relational: Spend time with your family, partner, and friends, go to a concert, get involved in a regular hobby or group-oriented sport.

Reflective: Journal, meditate, listen to music, go for a walk, do deep breathing exercises, read, etc.

General Health: Get seven to nine hours of sleep per night, drink lots of water, eat nutritious, whole foods.

CHAPTER 11 ACTIVITY

In what ways can you take care of yourself?

Build a daily routine that you can follow. Start small so you can build the capacity for this kind of self-care without becoming overwhelmed at the outset. Below you'll find instructions on how to get going in four steps.

1. List the components of your weekly self-care routine or goal. Keep this list online or near an accessible calendar. Answer the following questions:

   a) What time does/will this routine take place?

   b) What is the duration of the total routine (30 min, 1 hour, 1.5 hours, etc.)?

   c) List what it will include and how much time you will dedicate to each part of the routine.

   d) After you've accomplished the routine, keep track of this accomplishment. If you only accomplish part of the routine, take note.

   e) Track how many days you can complete your routine in one month and which parts of the routine you complete. This will get easier over time. Also, note which activities in the routine you follow through on and which are most challenging for you.

2. Create accountability! Share your routine with friends and see if they would like to participate with you. This will be an experiment. Let them know that you can hold each other accountable and share insights throughout the process. Also, let them know you'll be calling them out on

social media with the commitment. You can use the tag *#thechangesbook* to track things across social media.

3. On social media, tag someone you think may be interested in the challenge.

   Ok, now go do it! Seriously!

4. Feel good about how you take care of yourself. We could use that enthusiasm, that forward momentum, in taking care of each other!

12

MEDITATION FOR THE INDIVIDUAL AND THE ORGANIZATION

There are a lot of misconceptions surrounding meditation. I've heard all kinds of comments. *"Isn't that for hippies?"* *"I suck at meditation. I tried it once and couldn't do it."* Or *"I can't just sit there; I need to be doing something."*

Often, this type of resistance gives way to curiosity, interest, and after some experimentation and dedicated practice, enjoyment and tangible benefits. That said, it may take a little time to find the kind of meditation that fits you. A common misconception about meditation is that there's a single form, that it only looks like one thing. Plenty of minds conjure an image of a person sitting quietly, eyes closed, legs crossed, trying not to think. (Good luck with not thinking, by the way.) The truth is there are many varieties of meditation.

I have tried my hand at a wide variety of meditation practices, from basic breathing exercises to guided meditation to qigong (氣功), a Chinese-based practice of held postures and slow movements related to energy cultivation.[44] I have found all of these meditation styles to be valuable in one way or another.

When working with individuals and organizations, meditation and mindfulness come up regularly. In this chapter, we'll explore why meditation is so important for both the individual and the organization.

You may still be asking, *"What is the point of meditation?"* It's a valid question, but be prepared for a flood of answers! In broad strokes, meditation has been shown to reduce stress, anxiety, and depression and to improve productivity. Check out the particulars:

MEDITATION FOR THE INDIVIDUAL

Meditation has an impact on the mind, body, and overall well-being. Here are some examples of how meditation impacts the individual.

- **Impact on Aging** – *A study at UCLA concluded that long-term meditators had less age-related atrophy of gray matter in the brain. The finding suggests a relationship between long-term meditation and a reduction in age-related brain tissue decline.*[45]

- **Management of Health Conditions** – *The Mayo Clinic cites meditation as having a positive impact on emotional well-being and helping people manage symptoms of asthma, high blood pressure, and heart disease, among others.*[46]

- **Impact on Depression, Anxiety, and Pain** – *In a meta-analysis at Johns Hopkins, researchers determined that* *meditation practices had an impact on depression, anxiety, and pain.*[47]

- **Meditation and Self-Control** – *A study in 2013 by three US universities suggested that meditation training can improve self-control and help with quitting smoking.*[48]

MEDITATION FOR THE ORGANIZATION

The impact of meditation on an organization can be significant. Implementing meditation can positively affect productivity, absenteeism, and the bottom line.

- **Impact on Absenteeism** – *According to an article by Harvard Health Publishing, employees struggling with depression lose an average of 27 days of work per year.*[49] *If we take into account all the evidence of meditation reducing depression, it stands to reason that offering or encouraging meditation practices to employees would improve absenteeism and ultimately save the company time and money.*

- **Impact on Disability** – *The World Health Organization states, that as of 2018, depression is the leading cause of disability worldwide.*[50] *Ignoring the benefits of meditation, especially in regard to disability reduction, could result in excessive and unnecessary costs to companies.*

- **Impact on Healthcare Costs and Productivity** – *Mindfulness programs in corporations are on the rise. The insurance giant, Aetna, reported that since instituting its*

mindfulness program, it has saved $2000 per employee
in healthcare costs and gained $3000 per employee
in productivity.[51]

- **Meditation is becoming more common in the workplace**
  – An article in TIME shows that more and more meditation
  and mindfulness programs are being implemented in the
  workplace, as benefits are more widely recognized.[52]

So, now you may be asking, *"Which meditation practice do I choose, and what tools are available?"* In my work, I see the best mindfulness or meditation activity as the one that most closely resonates with each individual (or organization). Again, you don't just have to sit cross-legged and pretend to be *"not thinking."* There are many styles of meditation available, the trick is experimenting and finding one that you can stick with. There are also other tools available to complement your meditative practice.

One meditation tool many of our clients enjoy is a device called MUSE: The Brain Sensing Headband™. This tool gives immediate feedback on brain activity through a synced app on your mobile device, so you can use it anywhere.

This device works by first calibrating your current brain state and basically assessing how active or calm it is. As brain activity naturally fluctuates, it is necessary to start off with a base reading. From there, you get to pick the length of meditation you prefer, ranging from three minutes to one hour. You then choose a scene to listen to (rainforest, beach, city park, etc.), which is associated with your meditation session. You receive feedback in the form of sound coming from your chosen scene. For example, if you choose the beach scene, you hear crashing waves when your brain is active and gentle waves when your brain is calm. When your brain is particularly at ease, you hear birds chirping.

When the session is over, you receive a detailed report of your meditation and your brain's activity level. The report is presented in an easy-to-read graph of the changing activity during the session. For a detailed account of the process see the website, www.choosemuse.com.[53]

WHY MUSE™ CAN BE HELPFUL TO THE INDIVIDUAL OR ORGANIZATION

- **Easy to Understand Feedback** – *The immediate feedback MUSE™ offers is unique when it comes to meditation. Meditation is an ongoing process and requires a lot of patience, which can be challenging for those accustomed to getting immediate results. MUSE™ takes practice, but offers a way to see the direction you are heading.*

- **Fun in Competition** – *Meditation is not generally competitive, and I'm not suggesting it should be. However, the reality is that plenty of corporate wellness programs lack employee engagement. As such, there is a push to make engagement more appealing. One potential solution is to integrate MUSE™ into a company's wellness program by allowing for programs similar to today's popular challenges regarding healthy eating, walking, or drinking water. For example, how about a challenge to achieve a 75 percent relaxation average either individually or among all participants over the course of a month?*

- **Measurable** – *For those individuals or organizations that want to see progress quantified, MUSE™ fits the bill. Gathering data over time allows you to see where you started and how far you've come. Such data could then be compared with data on absenteeism, productivity, or engagement to reveal insights.*

- **An Introduction to Meditation** – *If you have never meditated, you may have developed certain assumptions about the practice. This device clears up some of the mystery. It allows a glimpse into what is possible with an optimized relationship between your mind and body. Enhancing our understanding of how our mind impacts other aspects of our health is a terrific opportunity for growth and development.*

Now before you start suspecting that I am working on commission for the company that manufactures The Muse device, let me clarify. While it is true that I have become a fan after seeing the product's value for me and many of my clients, the bigger point here is that any tool that offers a good introduction to meditation should be on your radar. As I mentioned in Chapter 11, there are other apps such as Calm and Headspace that help ease you into meditation. Remember, it may take some experimentation to determine what tools and practices are right for you or your organization.

CHAPTER 12 ACTIVITY

As I have already mentioned, the best meditation practice is the one that resonates most personally with each practitioner. It may take some experimentation to discover which practice best fits. Below, you'll find a chart with meditation options as well as where to learn more about them. I recommend experimenting with one type of practice daily for at least two weeks before deciding how you feel about it. I have only suggested a few types of meditation. There are many out there. Do some research and see if any others appeal to you. Keep track of the meditation types you discover along the way and your opinion of each. Have fun!

Meditation Type	Where to Look
Qigong	Search online for qigong teachers in your area. These directories may also be helpful: • https://www.qigonginstitute.org/directory • http://www.americantaichi.net/TaiChiQigongClass.asp
Seated (Vipassana)	There are many guided meditations online. This is a good directory: • http://www.dharma.org/teachers
Transcendental Meditation™	It is usually necessary to take a course in this type of meditation first, as there are very specific instructions. For more information: • https://www.tm.org/

Meditation Type	Where to Look
Muse Meditation Device	For more information and to order a Muse Meditation Device online: • www.choosemuse.com
Device Apps – i.e. Calm, Headspace, etc.	There are many apps you can find on your device. Some are free. I recommend Calm and Headspace.

GUTS

*"I like it when a flower or a little tuft
of grass grows through a crack of
concrete. It's so fuckin' heroic."*

—*George Carlin*

Sometimes it might seem like all the important factors are in place. We have insight, emotional balance, and good, healthy habits, but there is something missing. We haven't yet been able to muster the courage to take the risk that has paralyzed us with indecision. Pushing back against our fears and embracing uncertainty may be the necessary step toward our best selves.

It takes courage to create change. Challenging our fears, asking ourselves questions that get right down to the root of those fears, includes some discomfort. This is where guts come in. Fortunately, courage can be developed. When we explore all of the hurdles in the way of creating the life we want, we find that some of them are ones that we've set up ourselves. We build courage when we can be truly honest with our fear, our history, and our intention. We get to choose which risks to take, but taking risks is important. Small risk-taking over time strengthens our initiative and steals our resolve to handle whatever may come our way. This section of the book will explore how moving beyond the challenges in place and creating the change we want takes guts.

13

LETTING GO OF FEAR

I once had a job with two primary roles: sales and account management. Early in my stint, I landed a lucrative prospect and arranged to chat with the clients over video regarding our company's proposal. Understanding that the deal was a great opportunity and that closing it would make a great impression on my boss, I grew more and more nervous as the day of the call approached. I reviewed our proposal and thought I had a firm handle on it, despite the anxiety. When the day arrived, I got on the conference call with my boss standing next to me. I began with some pleasantries and launched into our presentation. It was progressing rather smoothly until about five minutes in, when I meant to turn to another detail and . . . blanked. I began to panic as I scrambled to find my place in the presentation. My silence seemed to last for 30 minutes. Finally, my boss couldn't take it anymore. He jumped in, took the reins of the presentation, and finished up the call while I sat there, utterly humiliated. Instead of stepping up to the challenge, gathering my thoughts, and acting in spite of my fears, I let the embarrassment totally consume me. This day, fear won.

From failures such as this one, I gained the life experience and perspective that underscore the lessons I now share with clients. Over the course of my career, I have traveled extensively to speak to a variety of organizations about leadership, organizational development, team effectiveness, mental health, and human development. The underlying intention is to improve awareness and, ultimately, organizational effectiveness.

Not too long after I choked on the conference call, I set out to speak to a group of about 35 people (or so I had been informed). I had presented to a group this size before and was relatively comfortable, but a few butterflies still fluttered. I was on my own and scheduled to speak for about two hours. I had practiced the content, set up some activities for the group, and built in time for interaction based on the number of people in the room. It felt like things would work out well.

As I entered what I'd assumed would be a small conference room, I encountered instead a full gymnasium packed with over 300 people, complete with stage and jumbotron. I gawked in disbelief as I watched a group finishing up a witty, engaging educational skit. A nice blend of action and humor, it sold their point with just enough seriousness. It was a tough act to follow and I was up next. When I blew it on the conference call, there were only five people involved. In this gym, I would be speaking to sixty times as many, and in person. Not only that, but the activities I had planned for 35 simply wouldn't translate with 300, which meant I had to throw out most of my notes and wing it. I still had my clothes on or else I would have thought it was a nightmare. Fear washed over me and my mind reeled with negative thoughts: *"You're not good enough. You're never prepared. Why even bother when you're destined to fail?"*

But before that voice got the best of me, I made a decision. I took a deep breath, realized I had an opportunity to shift my state of mind, and got up on the stage. I took a risk. Standing in front of the crowd, sweat beading on my forehead, I decided that the best way to overcome my nerves was to address them directly. I spoke candidly to the audience about my desire to engage them, and even a little about my doubts. After a bit of self-deprecation and a couple of laughs, we got started.

I spent the next two hours wandering through the crowd with a microphone like an energetic talk show host. I sought out connections with individuals in an attempt to change the vibe in the room, to make it more intimate so that it matched my original expectations. Things didn't go as planned, but because I didn't panic, they didn't end in disaster. In fact, they went pretty well.

Afterward, I felt invigorated, as if I had conquered something. The best part was all the feedback I received from audience members about how natural I was at speaking and that I didn't appear nervous at all, despite my admission. I laughed inwardly as I smiled, nodded, and shook hands. This was the first time I realized how much I loved speaking and training with large groups. I pushed past my fear, expanded my experience, and opened myself up to a new source of joy.

In my work with individuals regarding professional fears, what often comes up is the fear of pursuing what is most meaningful to them. This fear is often expressed in defeatist inner monologue. *"There are no jobs available." "The market is too saturated." "I don't have the credentials."* While some of these fears may be rooted in actual truth, I believe that it is imperative to recognize your own *perceptions* of such impediments before all else. Letting go of our reservations or limiting beliefs is the first step in overcoming our fears. A limiting belief is one that holds us back from taking positive action. We can't eliminate fear entirely, but we can choose to act, despite the fear. By making a practice of such fear-defying action, we develop our ability to respond appropriately. I'm sure you can think of time when you didn't act because of doubts about your readiness or your abilities or your education—in sum, your self-worth. These doubts bog us down and mire us in stagnation. Change needs motion to manifest itself. Doubts, reservations, and defeatist tendencies all function as inertia.

Taking the focus off of fear and choosing to act instead can be liberating. When considering change in your professional life, you may hear certain fears echo in your head or you may hear in the discouraging comments of others their own projected fears (if you'll indulge me in a little armchair analysis). Do any of the following fears sound familiar?

- *There isn't enough (work, money, opportunity etc.) to make the change worth it.*
- *Other people are better at this than I am.*
- *All others in my field are competitors.*
- *I'm not really a leader.*

Now consider what would happen if you, merely as an experiment, flipped those thoughts inside out:

- *There is an abundance of work available.*
- *My unique approach/personality/background will prove a benefit that others will recognize.*
- *Other people in my field can be my collaborators.*
- *Which leadership characteristics do I have and which can I improve.*

Changing a belief or shifting perspective creates a path to progress. This shift in perspective can, of course, be applied to a whole array of fears. Fear inhibits progress in several ways:

- *Inhibits creativity*
- *Reduces insight and limits understanding of alternative perspective*
- *Directs us toward undesired actions*

This last point deserves special attention. Fear can certainly be a motivator, but what kind of motivator? Often, fear triggers reactivity (remember the importance of response instead of reaction), which may not be in line with what you truly want for yourself. If you are unsure how to determine if your motivation is a reaction or a response, see Chapter 1 (The 4 R's).

Taking steps, even small steps, in the direction of a change you want to pursue is the best course of action. It's easy to say, *"You just have to decide to let go of your fear,"* but actually doing it is something else. Letting go of fear takes practice. There are always opportunities for decisive action. An immediate push-back against fear is always available to you. Creating a regular, consistent practice that promotes empowerment can help reduce fear. Practice taking small risks in regular increments.

For example, if you seek to improve your business and challenge your introversion, a natural first step would be to attend networking events on a regular basis. I once worked with a client who was going through a career change. Let's call this person Robin. When we started working together, Robin had been in a career for about a decade and had achieved some success. She had received praise from on high for her work ethic and her ability to organize projects, perform tasks efficiently, and solve complex problems. Much of Robin's work was not interpersonal, however. She had never been compelled to address her natural shyness. She was in the midst of pushing back on her social fears, in part so that she could take a leap into a new career. She wasn't sure what this new career would be at the time, but she knew she wanted something different, something that would push her toward self-improvement while making use of her strengths and talents.

She had a strong network of colleagues and friends, but due to her shyness, she had put off using them as a resource. She came to the point where she needed to leverage her network to move forward in the process, learn about opportunities, and get advice regarding new areas where her talents may thrive. Even though *"networking"* was the last thing she wanted to do, she knew that her city had a great, active scene of professionals and that she could get some excellent introductions if she pursued more connections.

We worked together on a strategy for making use of her network that pushed her just outside her comfort zone. We explored how she could show up at more networking events. This created a way to practice pushing back on her fear regularly, thus reducing it.

At first we explored a low-stakes way to do this is by setting a goal of talking to just one stranger for five minutes at each event. Over time, the fear of networking subsided and she was able to leverage connections that helped her create a great transition into a new career that she loved.

Overcoming professional fears opens the way to new opportunity and possibility. Letting go of fear is empowering, and empowerment should be part of any change you're seeking. If you choose to face a professional fear, be prepared because there will be repercussions, which may include:

- *New awareness about which direction to take*

- *Career change*
- *Promotion*
- *Retirement*
- *A decision to return to school*
- *Temporary stress*
- *Increased confidence*
- *Disruption of routine*
- *Questions (perhaps even skepticism) from others*

You'll notice that not all the bulleted items above may be immediately positive. That's okay. While addressing a fear may create a temporary disturbance, the long-term outcome will be advantageous.

CHAPTER 13 ACTIVITY

Here's an exercise to help you evaluate a particular fear, understand it better, address it more effectively, and move on. First, identify one of your fears AND write out a brief description of it. Next, take the time to answer each question below. Finally, apply the action!

FOUR STEPS FOR ADDRESSING THIS FEAR

1. **Is there a particular belief that you hold that is connected to this fear?**

2. **What specifically do you want that your fear is hindering?** If you figure out where the fear comes from and what it is connected to, you may gain new awareness about how to approach it. If this fear didn't exist, how could you attain what you want?

3. **Once you understand what you want, start taking small steps in that direction.** Do research to determine which steps to take along the path that you've set for yourself. For instance, if you want to start a new career, but fear losing the security of the job you currently tolerate, consider taking this initial step. Brainstorm industries, fields, and specializations that you'd like to move into. List the five that interest you most. Next, identify anyone in your network who may work in those fields or know someone who does, and set up interviews to learn more. If this feels

too overwhelming, that's OK. There are other strategies you can employ to move toward your goal. Another option is to consider working with a coach, therapist, or mentor. For more information about how to find someone to work with, visit Part Two of the book.

4. **Set small, achievable goals you can attain and build on.** Put into place a daily routine that will guide you toward overcoming the fear. Prove to yourself that your fear can be conquered, and your belief in what is possible will grow. Identify two actions that counter your fear. For example, if your fear involves starting a business, set a goal to have a conversation with, at least, one successful entrepreneur a week in order to educate yourself and develop a realistic, but ambitious plan. Setting small, consistent daily goals that counter your fear is one effective way to diminish its power.

14

CULTIVATING SELF-DISCIPLINE

Discipline and motivation are often linked. When motivation wanes, it is often discipline that picks up the slack.

I was told by a meditation teacher once that it's not about *how well* you meditate, but simply *that* you meditate. It's the time on the mat, not how you did on the mat. It's the practice in and of itself. Sometimes, regardless of what kind of change we are seeking, building the discipline toward change is the most important piece.

Over the years, I've experimented with different diets. One that I was particularly fond of was a month-long, restricted diet called the Whole30®.[54] This was definitely an act of discipline for me, as food is a significant weakness. In case you are wondering, pizza and donuts are not part of the regimen, a significant sacrifice. Most of the time when I explore ways of eating, exercise routines, or other practices, I find the process eye-opening in a variety of ways. There are always discoveries along the way when pursuing a regimen that builds self-discipline.

In martial arts, I have found a practice that is highly conducive to building self-discipline. Even after 12 years of regular practice, I still find new ways to integrate this discipline into my life. While there are many activities, sports, and passions that will help you develop discipline, I think adopting some kind of physical or movement-based practice is particularly helpful because it cultivates greater body-awareness and shows us that we are capable of pushing past more discomfort, both physical and mental, than we think we're capable of. Plus, a routine of physical activity increases energy levels and reduces stress. As such, practicing discipline in terms of physical activity translates especially well to cultivating self-discipline in other aspects in our lives, as we'll see in this chapter.

I also witness the virtue of self-discipline in the lives of the clients I work with. Whether the client is a company or an individual, discipline enters early in the conversation.

For instance, I once worked with a woman (let's call her Julie) who was trying to cut down on her alcohol consumption. Julie was a professional who owned a small business and was rather successful. With a good network of friends and an array of interests, she seemed to be well-functioning, yet privately she feared that her alcohol consumption was becoming problematic and therefore wanted to address it. One of the ways we worked together was to explore the discipline she employed in her various life domains (career, relationships, fitness, etc.) By building discipline in different parts of her life, she was able to generate more willpower in service of her primary goal, reducing her alcohol intake. She set about developing discipline in ways she enjoyed: going to the gym, spending time in her faith community, and practicing meditation. These disciplined acts then reinforced her capacity to be more disciplined elsewhere.

If we build a skill or habit in one area of our life, it crosses over to other areas.

When we build discipline in our sleep habits, for instance, it impacts our ability to exercise regularly. Specifically, when we are well-rested, our motivation to exercise increases. In general, practicing discipline helps to strengthen our willpower, which can then be applied advantageously across our various life domains.

There is plenty of evidence for the positive impact of self-discipline across many aspects of the human experience, including developing good habits, physical health, financial stability, etc. Regardless of one's age, there are major advantages to practicing discipline. According to a longitudinal study by The Positive Psychology Center at the University of Pennsylvania, self-discipline accounted for twice as much variance as IQ in the final grades of eighth grade students.[55] These findings suggest that one of the major reasons students fall short is not due to their IQ, but to their lack of self-discipline. The self-discipline that accounts for higher grades will most likely have a significant impact on a child's ability to be successful later in life.

A study in *The Journal of Applied Developmental Psychology* showed that implementing a school-based martial arts program had a positive impact on children's cognitive self-regulation, an aspect of self-discipline.[56]

The impact of discipline is not just found in kids. In a study by Washington University's Department of Psychology, it was found that enhancing self-discipline and self-concept may improve subjective memory in older adults.[57]

In addition, according to a study in *The Journal of Depression and Anxiety*, low self-discipline has been associated with anxiety and depressive disorders.[58]

If only to drive home the point, I will state it once more: discipline is critical in the creation of any positive change. I continue to emphasize discipline because it is a *"meta-skill,"* a skill that helps build other skills. If we cultivate self-discipline, it impacts not only our ability to create the kind of changes we want, but also the skills that pertain to various aspects of our lives, as research shows.

5 TIPS FOR GROWING SELF-DISCIPLINE

1) **Take your time** – Building any new habit takes time. Taking small steps over time is the best recipe for success. Remember, creating significant change is a process.

2) **SMART goals** – Goals that are the easiest to keep track of and the most likely to be achieved are Specific, Measurable, Attainable, Realistic, and Timely. Even though you may be familiar with this framework for goal setting in general, pay close attention when applying it to building discipline. Use this framework for instituting and keeping track of disciplined behavior. It will lead you to greater confidence and success overall.

3) **Find your practice** – Building self-discipline will be most effective if the practice is something you find particularly enjoyable. Think of this step as a springboard in the

process. Commit yourself to a practice that is simpler than, yet related to, the one in which you are trying to build discipline and you will generate momentum toward ultimate success.

4) **Record your process** – Explore what it feels like (the ups and the downs) to create a new discipline in your life. This will be helpful when you examine what works and what doesn't. As you move forward, take note of your accomplishments and challenges.

5) **Practice creating routine** – Practicing any kind of routine, even if it is outside the context of your goal, will help foster the right mindset. There are opportunities to create new routines every day; take advantage of them. The discipline you build in one area will transfer to the areas of your life where you really want it to be!

CHAPTER 14 ACTIVITY

Ready to take action?

How have you created self-discipline in your life?

Complete the activities below to understand smaller victories and build new forms of discipline.

In this chapter, create your own discipline journal! Think you're not disciplined? Think again! We all have this capacity; it's just a matter of strengthening the right muscles. Follow the instructions below.

1) In which area of your life would you like to create more self-discipline?

2) What steps can you take toward reaching this goal? For example, if your primary discipline goal is:
   "Arrive 30 minutes earlier to work."

Factors associated with this goal may include sleep, diet, scheduling activities the night before, etc. Write down all of these factors and create a disciplined practice for each. The more success you have with the factors, the easier it will be for you to ultimately reach your primary goal. Track the times you performed these activities successfully and unsuccessfully. By doing so, you'll get a better sense of what your strengths are and what is holding you back.

15

CHALLENGING PERSPECTIVES AND MAINTAINING GROUND

I f you've been doing the activities through the chapters, good work! Taking the time to carefully evaluate yourself and all the dimensions of your life will help you identify what's keeping you stuck and preventing you from reaching your goals. I understand that this process can be a bit overwhelming, so perhaps it's time for a break. No activities for this chapter. Instead, I offer here a couple of stories and some tips from my years of experience as an organizational consultant, psychotherapist, and professional coach. The common theme of these stories is courage. Similarly, all of the tips take guts to implement.

INTROSPECTION: A BARRIER TO ENTRY

I saw a prime example of the courage it takes, not just to acknowledge, but also to actively work on our weaknesses, while working with Rob, a high-performing executive. Rob had a decorated military career, was in excellent physical shape, had an accomplished education, and excelled at most everything he engaged in. As a high performer, he shot up the corporate ladder. At one point, he received some feedback: if he were to continue moving into higher leadership roles at his current company, he'd need to show greater empathy for his co-workers and improve his people skills, overall. In other words, he'd need to raise his emotional intelligence. He had heard this kind of thing before, but had always dismissed it as touchy/feely and a waste of time. For the first time in his career, though, this very development was the barrier to entry for his upward trajectory.

At the beginning of our work together, Rob and I explored some of his history. We looked at how he had gone about achieving so much. He had always been hyper-focused on results. His default assessment of everything was: how does this affect the bottom line?

We talked about his ambition and where it came from. When Rob was a teenager, his father died. As a way to deal with the pain and carry some of the financial burden for his family, Rob committed himself to excellence. He believed his no-excuses attitude had served him well, and in many ways, he was right.

Rob didn't let anything get in his way, including people. The problem was that, given the high bar he always set for himself, he had a difficult time adjusting his expectations for others. He didn't hide his disappointment and frustration with his co-workers and developed a reputation for being impossible to please.

He believed that if he developed patience and sensitivity, it would come at the cost of the very traits to which he owed his success. We explored how he could challenge this *"zero-sum"* notion. Since Rob had cultivated this attitude for some time, the process of replacing it with a different mindset would require some heavy lifting. This is where courage comes in.

For anyone to challenge a long-established pattern of perceiving the world and engaging with others, courage is paramount. No matter what kind of person you are (overachiever or underachiever), no matter your beliefs or attitudes, summoning that willingness to look at yourself with greater objectivity can be an intense, daunting process.

Through our process together, we focused on gathering insight and then applying it in the workplace. Rob had plenty of opportunity to apply new perspectives and ways of engaging with people, as he led many teams and projects. By asking more questions, engaging in more personal conversations, practicing empathy, eliciting feedback, and tracking the changes he was experiencing, he discovered the numerous benefits of relationship-building. What began as a pursuit to check a box became a sincere commitment to improve himself.

I witnessed a tremendous shift in how Rob approached work and people at his company. He was able to reduce his frustration with others, increase collaborative efforts with individuals and teams, and ultimately gain greater recognition for his improved leadership skills. These efforts also resulted in a couple of major promotions (with considerable salary increases) in less than a year.

As it relates to performance, it's no surprise that Rob succeeded. He had the guts to evaluate himself at the core and examine which parts of his personality were serving him and which were detrimental. This 180 degree turn is what I found so inspiring. It's a lesson we can all learn from.

~

Here are a handful of general principles related to courage that also help us reduce stress, accomplish goals, and build our ability to adapt. I see these principles in practice when individuals and organizations are most successful in creating positive change. You may see some familiar content here, but anything important bears repeating.

1) **Push yourself further than you think you're capable of going** – Going the extra mile can greatly improve your overall effectiveness. Try this in different areas of your life to boost confidence in relationships, fitness, finance, and career. Just add a bit extra to all that you do (i.e. ten more minutes at the gym, an extra half hour of sleep, an extra half hour of work, helping a coworker when you don't need to, or doing something for a loved one before they ask). You are capable of more than you think.

    When you reach that point when you are ready to give up, push yourself over the hump. Dig down to the depths of yourself and find the energy required. Need some motivation? Keep in mind that authentic motivation requires REPS – Reflection, Evaluation, Persistence, and Significance. (See Chapter 2 for details.)

2) **Be kind & offer support** – There are injustices all around us. We see this on a large scale when we watch the news and witness war, deprivation, exploitation, and other forms of inhumanity. We see this in our daily lives too: at work when someone is isolated or picked on, at social events when someone is excluded, or in our family gatherings

when someone is left out. These are all opportunities for you to stand up to defend the rights of others.

Some of the most successful people I know have an uncanny ability to offer consistent support and kindness so that others may grow and develop. When they build up people around them, it creates a network of successful individuals, and these individuals are likely to acknowledge the support they received. When the original supporter needs support, they often have people lining up to offer it because of the kindness they have spread.

Hold a door open for someone, leave a generous tip, express to someone their importance to you, or recognize how someone has gone above and beyond expectations. Kindness is also an act of discipline: the more you practice, the more it becomes second nature.

3) **Be cautious about making assumptions (especially about people)** – You know what they say about the word *assume*... I hope. Our assumptions of each other often prevent us from truly connecting. Check your assumptions when they crop up. Are they based on a current perception? Are they informed by previous experience? Or are they based on secondhand experience or mere conjecture? If you are unsure how to test your assumptions about someone in particular, try communicating openly with the person and expressing your need for clarity. Asking for clarity shows that you are interested and curious, which is usually appreciated.

4) **Be uncomfortable & take risks** – We cannot predict the future. We won't know how exactly our decisions will

impact us or others until we act. Taking risks in business, career, or relationships is often a prerequisite for growth. Of course, understanding the risk is important too. Prevent *"paralysis by analysis"* by acting. It's okay to be uncomfortable. This is how we grow. I had a professor in graduate school, one of my best mentors to date, Dr. Jack Mulgrew. He ran a class on group therapy, which focused on being mindful of your present experience and expressing it authentically. He said something once that has always stuck with me:

"If you are not on the edge of your seat sweating, you are not working hard enough."

His point was that times of discomfort, uncertainty, or insecurity often set the stage for action. As such, we should move toward them, not away from them.

5) **Take on your fears & examine your shadows** – How are your fears getting in the way of growth? Challenging your fear and moving past it means facing it head-on. For example, if you fear you'll never get a raise, then maybe you should seize the opportunity to make a convincing case for it and bring it to your boss. Or perhaps, through this examination, you realize that you don't deserve a raise.

Just as each and every one of us has flattering aspects, we all have aspects that inspire more shame than pride. Summon the courage to evaluate these facets of your personality. Some refer to them as darker sides or shadows, not only because they are often negative, but also because they have managed to escape the light of observation. Since these aspects are often repressed, they may not be immediately identifiable.

Third-party assistance from a therapist or coach can be particularly helpful in bringing these blind spots to your attention. Evaluating your fears, weaknesses, biases, unhealthy habits, self-defeating tendencies, and/or other unsavory aspects of yourself can also lead to true insight and personal development.

6) **Embrace your passions** – Do you know what you are passionate about? In no small way, your passions define who you are. Don't let your passions come second. Build a life around them and watch yourself flourish! In my work with coaching clients I often field the question, *"Is it too late to go back to doing something I love?"*

I see so much regret from folks who waited to embrace their passions and put to use their greatest strengths. Certainly, it is never too late to go back or to make change. In this respect, paying attention to your intuition can lead to lots of opportunity.

7) **Focus on building your strengths** – We often think we need to improve our weaknesses to the exclusion of all else. While there is insight to be gained from understanding our challenges and addressing them, improving our strengths is a greater predictor of success. According to research by Gallup, identifying our top strengths and building on them offers the greatest return on investment.[59] This is found to be true in many areas in life, including work, recreation, and interpersonal relationships.

8) **Establish congruence between intentions and actions and lead by example** – Take time to understand what you value. Express your values in how you live your life. If you are unsure, consider working with a coach or therapist.

Have you ever dealt with bosses, teachers, or mentors, who seemed to act differently from what they professed? How did this sit with you? I imagine it was hard to take them seriously when they said one thing and did another. To be a better partner, leader, parent (to be a better human being, for that matter), you need to exemplify what you claim is important. Your actions need to be in alignment with your stated values and beliefs.

Our intentions, thoughts, and plans are pivotal, but they are only part of the change we seek. Knowing is not half the battle. It is less than half. I have seen many people in my work and personal life who have plenty of insight, but fail to thrive because they don't apply it. True change happens when insight is applied through action. Remember this quote:

"You are what you do, not what you say you'll do." —*C.G. Jung*

9) **Challenge authority and ask questions** – Just because someone is in a position of authority doesn't mean that they are in a position of truth. I am grateful for this lesson, which was ingrained in me at an early age. Thanks, Mom. If something doesn't resonate with you, then ask questions, do your research, and discover the truth for

yourself. Remember, it is okay to ask questions! If you
don't understand something, or if you want to challenge it,
then do so. The longer you remain uncertain or ignorant,
the longer you are at a disadvantage. You already know this
intuitively. Consider reflecting on a time when you've felt
uncertain, undecided, or generally clueless about a situation or concept. Remember that uncomfortable, scared,
or frustrated feeling that you felt in your body? To reduce
your own anxiety, be curious and ask questions.

10) **Embrace abundance** – What we focus on becomes a part
of our mindset. A negative mindset (i.e. a focus on what
is lacking, what isn't working, what we fear, what isn't
available to us, etc.) can be countered with a simple shift in
perspective. We get to choose how we make meaning and
interpret situations. What if we convinced ourselves that
there is plenty of opportunity, customers, resources, love,
support, money, etc. out there for us and everyone else?
What if we emphasized collaboration instead of competition? I think you'd be surprised at how much better you'd
feel and consequently how many opportunities would
present themselves. If you're skeptical, test it out. Try
assuming that there is abundance, and see what happens.
Granted, this takes guts. I admit it's not easy. Given the
social, economic, political, and environmental challenges
we face every day such a shift in perspective requires
serious intention and maybe even some suspension of
disbelief. To realize the full potential of this perspective,
you must wholeheartedly embrace it. In our pursuit of

positive change, embracing abundance is one of the most useful tools available to us.

~

The first story in the chapter showed the courage it takes to look inward and make necessary changes. This next story explores the courage it takes to persist, even in despair. In my work, I have met individuals who, in the midst of internal battles, have shown a resilience that continues to inspire. This next story exemplifies that kind of resilience.

MOVING FORWARD

In 2012, I was working at a community mental health center as a therapist and crisis worker. The crisis work consisted of responding to various mental health emergencies in the community. I was often called in to offer help to people at their lowest point; some were overcome by great emotional pain, some were wrestling with delusions, and some were threatening violence. This kind of work takes a toll. In addition to work stress, I was dealing with the recent death of someone close to me and was feeling emotionally drained.

On a particularly tough day, I received a message that a student at the local high school was threatening to kill himself. I went out to do a safety check, an assessment of the situation to ensure that the individual doesn't have the means or the intention to do harm to him/herself or others. Aiming to do my best,

I had to chase away doubts that I would be able to offer the kid much value given the state I was in.

At the school, a counselor introduced me to the student (Andy) and then left us alone to talk. Feeling trapped by circumstances, Andy had convinced himself that suicide was his only option. We discussed life in general, the pressures of school, relationships, and family. We also talked about what was going well in his life, friends he had, his love of art and the college experience he looked forward to. Even with these positive things in his life, he had lost hope. His inability to identify the source of his despair only compounded it. Though I wasn't sure if Andy was hiding the real cause of his pain or not, I could tell that his emotions were real, and in a sense, at least, I could relate to him right there in that moment.

After what seemed like an eternity of silence as I tried to come up with the perfect thing to say—something that would let him know he's not alone in feeling overwhelmed by emotions, but also in a way that respected his unique experience—I realized that the best I could do would still fall short. So, I just looked at him and told him that sometimes we have to just keep moving forward. I don't know if it sounded as lame then as it does now, but in the moment it seemed true. I think I was talking to myself as much as I was talking to him. We discussed the difficult truth that sometimes the answers, advice, or outcomes we want or think we need simply aren't available. We talked about how in such situations, you need to keep pushing toward the changes ahead. Actually being in motion can also be a helpful distraction. It generates energy and reduces the feeling of being stuck that accompanies sadness. In time, moving physically helps us move on emotionally.

This is where having guts enters the picture. Sometimes acting courageously is about simply moving, even if you don't know which way is *"forward."* In this way, courage intersects with faith. This is another example of some of the seven dimensions converging as part of the change process.

A couple of days later, there was a knock on my office door. It was the school counselor dropping by to tell me that Andy was doing better and to drop off a small package. I opened it up and found a piece of wood carved in the shape of an arrow with a message neatly burned into it: *"keep moving forward."*

CHAPTER 15 ACTIVITY

Just reflect and enjoy.

ENVIRONMENTS

*"You are the average of the five people
you spend the most time with."*

—*Jim Rohn*

You are the product of your environment. For clarity, in this context, environment includes many aspects of your experience: workplace, home, city, community, friendships, geographical location, culture, etc. All of these environments influence us to a greater or lesser degree. The people, places, and things we surround ourselves with impact our ability to create and maintain change.

If you feel as though you've worked through all of your patterns, challenges, and bad habits and still can't reach the goals you seek, consider studying your environment. You have the choice to fill your life with people, places, and things that build you up or those that undermine you, feed doubt, or otherwise impede your development. Spending more time in nurturing environments increases your likelihood for creating the positive change you seek.

16

INSPIRATION AND ENGAGEMENT IN THE WORKPLACE

"*If you only had five hundred words to share, what wisdom would you want to pass on to humanity?*" This was the prompt I was to answer for an article I once wrote for a website called *Inspire Me Today.*[60]

Of course, it is a complicated question, but it was fun to contemplate. My answer consisted of ways to build positive qualities, among them courage, congruence, and inspiration. In the end, though, I was left wondering, inspiration is so fleeting . . . how do we hold on to it, how do we make it last?

Since we spend a majority of our time in the workplace, it seems fitting to tailor the question accordingly: How do we make inspiration last at work? A corollary concern arises: How do we enhance engagement? These are concerns for any organization, regardless of industry, size, and location.

This section of the book is about how our environment impacts our ability to create the positive change we seek. If our workplace (one of our most consistent environments) can be optimized for success, it will create forward momentum that can affect positive change in other areas of our lives. And we all are at our best, at work and at home, when we are inspired.

Whether we're talking about a Global 500 company or a local, family-owned business, the means to inspire are the same. One especially promising way to engage and inspire is to align values. Such alignment requires accountability at the leadership level, by which I mean that the person at the top has to be willing to receive and act upon feedback from employees.

Certainly, inspiration is a challenge to sustain. As you probably know from experience, it is impossible for us to remain in a constant state of inspiration. It simply takes too much energy. But even considering our natural constraints, the idea of inspiring employees on a more regular basis should be of primary concern to companies. Again, critical to the matter is the workplace environment, which, if not vigilantly monitored, can foster fear, mistrust, and resentment. Companies must create an environment that fosters inspiration on a daily basis.

Here are four tips to inspire employees and encourage employee engagement:

1. **Employee turnover is expensive, unproductive, and challenging.** Keeping employees engaged and enthusiastic will reduce employee turnover and ultimately reduce costs and lost productivity for the company. According to Gallup, a whole slew of major performance outcomes are connected to engagement, including profitability, productivity, and customer ratings.[61] Managers can elicit greater engagement from their employees by simply setting the examples themselves. When managers focus on building trust, rapport, and communication, they keep their employees emotion-

ally engaged, thus driving results. Follow-up evaluations of managers may be necessary to ensure effectiveness.[62]

2.   **For most employees, one of the essential components of a positive work experience is feeling appreciated.** By consistently acknowledging employees' contributions, leaders can improve employees' experiences and reduce the likelihood of turnover.[63]

3.   **Make sure management is leading with inspiration.** In an IBM-conducted study about leadership in which 1700 chief executives from 64 countries were interviewed, it was found that inspirational leadership was one of three primary traits identified with steering organizations effectively.[64] According to best-selling author Carmine Gallo, there are a number of ways leaders can inspire, including encouraging potential, reinforcing optimism, and inviting participation.[65]

4.   **Understanding the relationship between a company's values and its employees' values is important.** One way to determine such a relationship is to move employees to positions that better utilize their strengths and are more closely aligned with their values. A glaring mismatch between employee and company values is likely to lead to either employee underperformance or employee departure. For example, if an employee values teamwork and believes that his/her employer does not approach problems collaboratively, the discrepancy will most likely diminish the employee's engagement. If the match is unclear, consider

bringing in consultants or coaches who can evaluate and help determine best options.

So, how does a company get leadership to understand the importance of employee engagement?

Human Resources departments and executives need to feel engaged in their work so they can experience the value of what they will be teaching to other leaders in the company. It's a top-down approach. Modeling the behavior that is expected organization-wide is crucial. To ensure that they are engaged, leaders must determine that their personal values are aligned with the company's and that their strengths and duties are in sync. When organizational leadership is disengaged, it is likely to impact company culture as a whole.

When there is congruence between a leader's personal values and those of the company, the workplace is usually much more inspiring for employees. For example, when a leader values giving back to the community and an organization establishes a strong philanthropic program, the leader tends to stay inspired and remain with the company. This seems relatively intuitive: if values match, then positive outcomes will result, but you may be surprised by how often this wisdom is neglected. One way to create this alignment is through crystal-clear communication. Often poor communication results in a whole host of negative consequences, including lack of accountability, finger-pointing among employees, indifference to customers, missed opportunities for innovation, and poor levels of collaboration. Mounting evidence underscores the importance of engagement, value alignment, and inspired employees in relation to business success.[66]

For example, according to a 2009 study by Towers Watson, companies whose workforce was assessed as *"highly engaged"* on the average improved operating income by 19 percent over a 12-month period. Companies found to have lower workforce engagement on the average saw a 32 percent decrease in operating income over the same period.[67]

For more data underscoring the value of addressing engagement and other human dynamic issues, see the extensive list of studies and statistics created by *The Social Workplace*.[68]

Now that we understand the primary importance of values in relation to engagement, we should dig a little deeper and ask: *"What does this mean?"* When considering value alignment, we need to first appraise our own values. Of course, articulating our values can be difficult. I have witnessed coaching clients, individuals as well as companies, struggle with identifying what is truly important to them. Working with a coach can be a great way to help explore your values if you are uncertain where to start.

What we value and what inspires us are unique parts of our reality. Take this story of inspiration, for example.

As I mentioned in Chapter 1, I visited Chile in 2009. On a scholarship from Rotary International's Group Study Exchange Program, I traveled down with a small group of professionals from various fields as part of a cross-cultural exchange with a partner country. Our group, representing western North Carolina, was to trade places with one from the central region of Chile, the Santiago area.

We attended numerous Rotary meetings with our Chilean partners to discuss our professions and how they differed culturally between the two countries. In addition to attending social events, we also took expansive tours of museums, schools, government buildings, and the occasional winery. It was a fantastic adventure, full of rich connections, and lots of learning.

One of the many advantages of this scholarship was that we could stay in our host country for up to a month and the scholarship would still pay for the flight home. I took advantage of this perk.

As my colleagues and friends departed for the States, I connected with an old friend. We traveled north, stopping in coastal towns as we made our way to the Atacama Desert.

This desert is the driest non-polar desert on the planet. Imagine a rugged Martian landscape—cracked riverbeds and jagged rocks—and in the distance, soft rolling hills, and beyond that, the big blue void of sky. That pretty much captures it. Because of the unique arid climate, lack of light pollution, and high altitude, this desert is one of the best locations on the planet for stargazing. When we arrived in town, we visited one of these observatories.

On the observatory tour, our guide presented a nifty device, a hand-held laser-pointer that had a reach of over one mile. To the human eye, this magic, little device created the illusion that it was actually touching the stars and constellations that we heard described in detail.

The guide, Diego, was in his mid-twenties, enthusiastic, friendly, and very knowledgeable. He had a passion for astronomy, and he was pumped about an upcoming trip. He would be heading north just a few days later and would finally get to the other side of the equator. There he would see something he had been hearing about since he was a boy—The Big Dipper!

If you live north of the equator, you are no doubt familiar with The Big Dipper. If you're like plenty of North Americans, it may be one of the only constellations that you know. Perhaps it was pointed out to you when you were a child. If so, it's likely you have been able to recognize it every time you look up into the night sky. This isn't the case for all our friends south of the equator. They have a different sky to gaze upon.

Diego's enthusiasm for something that to my friend and me seemed so commonplace was both amusing and touching. In a trip full of unforgettable experiences, this memory stands out. It made me consider how vastly one person's experience differs from another's. What we take for granted due to overexposure, others may see as a sort of miracle.

I remember Diego fondly. He taught me a great lesson in perspective, motivation, and inspiration. Here was a person truly engaged in his work. He had found the right match between his passions and career.

This encounter brought to mind a number of important questions.

- *How can our view of something (both figuratively and literally) impact our reality?*
- *How does our perspective affect the things we take for granted?*
- *How can we capitalize on the opportunity to shift our perspective and ignite inspiration?*
- *How can we find opportunity to match more of our passion within our career?*
- *How would a new career add more inspiration, engagement, and enjoyment to our day?*

These are questions I am grateful to ask myself and others on a regular basis. I hope you are able to consider them deeply and honestly.

CHAPTER 16 ACTIVITY

This chapter's activity is more of a reflection. Consider answering the following questions and then applying some of the insight you gain to your workplace experience. You can draw on the research from this chapter as well as on your experience, insight, and understanding of your environment. The hope is that, based on your insights, you can show your company how improving inspiration in your workplace will add value all across your organization. Answer the six questions below and take action!

1) **Is your current level of engagement in your work high, moderate, or low?** Describe what inspires and engages you as well as what drains your energy.

2) **What are three values you share with your company?** There are many values to choose from. Examples include:
   » *Meaningful feedback*
   » *Teamwork*
   » *Opportunity for learning*
   » *Cause-based work*
   » *Aesthetics of workplace*
   » *Quality of product or service*
   » *Consistent financial growth opportunity*

3) **What are three values you and your company don't share?**

4) **List three things that you take part in that inspire you?**

5) What can you change in your environment to build more inspiration?

6) What action will you take to influence your environment?

17

THE BEST LISTENER
AT WORK

Most of us understand the importance of good communication skills, but all too often we forget that half of good communication is good listening. Think of your workplace. Think of all the people you encounter throughout the day: customers, clients, boss, co-workers, etc. You probably have a variety of feelings about all of these people. I bet you can remember the ones who are good listeners. I also bet you know how you feel when someone is truly present with you and shows that you have his or her attention. Doesn't it feel good to know that your voice has found an audience? Given the power of this feeling, it's a wonder that listening skills aren't more of a focus in and out of our workplaces. They are powerful skills to build.

In the fast-paced, high-demand jobs so many of us have these days, good listening skills, unfortunately, have become something of a novelty. Our time is precious because of ever-impending deadlines, constant distractions, and the general stress that pervades the workplace. If you commit to being a better listener at work, you will likely notice some of these challenges subside.

So, how might listening skills impact your workplace environment or any environment for that matter? Consider your experience now. Do you feel heard at work? What do you notice about people who are sincerely present with you when you are speaking, as opposed to those who are anxious to move on to the next task or are simply waiting for their turn to speak? When someone is really present with you, it makes communication easier. You may feel more connected, more at ease. You're also more likely to get your message across clearly. Good listening skills reduce miscommunication.

Think of the best listener you know. What if you were that kind of expert listener for everyone else? How would it impact your workplace experience if co-workers knew that when they spoke to you, they could count on you to pay close attention to them? What if they knew that they could count on you to not misinterpret, misread, manipulate, or otherwise misconstrue their message?

Excellent listening skills go a long way, particularly if you are a leader. Being able to communicate, understand, and connect with your employees is a crucial component of effective leadership. According to a study in *The Journal of Occupational Health*, it was concluded that *"... psychological stress reactions were lower in subordinates who worked under supervisors with high listening skills."*[69]

In another study cited by the journal, *Small Group Research*, results indicated *"... that emergent leaders typically display more effective listening skills than other members."*[70]

The research on the positive effects of good listening skills supports what I have consistently found to be true in my business consulting work. Leaders often ask me how to support their team. I respond to their question with one of my own, *"How often do you ask your employees the following kinds of questions?"*

> *What can I do to support your success?*
>
> *What feedback would be most helpful for you?*
>
> *What feedback can you offer me on my leadership?*
>
> *How is my leadership either boosting your success or impeding it?*
>
> *How well am I communicating or leading? What would make either one more effective for you?*

Leaders are surprised when they discover how a simple intervention, such as asking better questions, can be so effective at resolving complex problems. Even though this is a simple change in behavior, any new way of approaching situations takes regular practice. (Stay tuned. You'll have the chance to do so at the end of this chapter.)

Over the years, I've witnessed a vast array of positive changes when leaders start asking these questions with consistency and sincerity. These questions offer the opportunity to engage in active listening and lead to productive conversations. Furthermore, this kind of dialogue directly engages employees, and as we discussed last chapter, engaged employees stick around and work more productively.

These kinds of questions are not limited to leadership or your work environment. Asking questions that convey your curiosity to others can be a great way to practice your listening skills. If this is a new strategy for you, my advice is to start with *what* and *how* questions because open-ended questions allow people the freedom to express whatever's on their mind. If being curious isn't your default, don't fret: you can cultivate curiosity through practice. By asking open-ended questions of others more regularly, you will soon see the benefits. The more people feel that they are being listened to and that their input is valued, the more value they will add.

A good strategy for remembering how to cultivate curiosity comes from a counseling orientation called Motivational Interviewing. This strategy is called OARS.[71] The acronym stands for:

- *Open-ended questions – asking questions that cannot be answered with a mere Yes or No.*
- *Affirmation – authentically acknowledging a part of the story that you understand, agree with, empathize with, or otherwise connect to.*
- *Reflection – checking in for clarification as well as encouraging further explanation.*
- *Summary – offer a recap of what you've heard, not verbatim, but a basic summary of the main points.*

Developing our ability to listen will impact all of our environments. Here are three more tips to improve your listening skills.

1) FOCUS

We sometimes get caught up in how we are going to respond to something while the other person is still speaking. Prematurely thinking of what to say next reduces your ability to thoroughly process what someone is saying. Attending to what someone is saying, without simultaneously focusing on how to respond, will create stronger communication. Remain focused on the present moment and thoroughly digest what is being said.

2) BREATHE

Often in the workplace (and in many environments) we are moving at what feels like a million miles a minute. This frantic pace minimizes our ability to fully take in information presented at any given juncture. Take a few moments to consciously breathe as you converse with someone. This practice will help you to be more present and process what they are saying more effectively. Before you speak, or when you are feeling overwhelmed, stop and take a deep breath. This may sound trivial, but this small step can do wonders. By reducing your stress and increasing your capacity to be in the present, you increase your ability to communicate. If you need additional help in slowing down and staying present, revisit the section on Nourishment and apply what you learned about mindfulness to the development of your listening skills.

3) WAIT

Our immediate default in conversation is to fill silence. I suggest resisting this urge. Even if you have something to say, by waiting a couple of extra seconds (or perhaps many), you allow for more ideas to flow on either end. This may sound obvious, but when you ask someone a question, it's important to give them time to respond. This means not jumping in to answer for them while they're formulating their ideas. We don't all process information at the same speed. Our discomfort with a sustained pause often disrupts those that may need a couple extra moments to gather their thoughts. Having good listening skills requires patience, and getting comfortable with silence is part of the drill.

CHAPTER 17 ACTIVITY

For the next couple of weeks, test some of the behaviors listed above. After you've had the opportunity to track your progress, reflect on what worked and what came most naturally to you. For noticeable results, you may have to practice one, two, or all three behaviors, at least 4 times a week for three weeks.

After you've practiced, answer the following questions:

- *How did the behaviors work, if they worked at all?*
- *What did you learn?*
- *How did you practice each behavior?*
- *How long did you practice each new behavior?*

Test your results. After a few weeks of practice, ask a few co-workers the following question:

HOW CAN I IMPROVE MY ABILITY TO LISTEN AND BE PRESENT?

Take note of their observations and suggestions. See what themes emerge and continue to practice.

Finally, don't forget to keep asking these questions:

What can I do to support your success?

What feedback would be most helpful for you?

What feedback can you offer me on my leadership?

How is my leadership either boosting your success or impeding it?

How well am I communicating or leading? What would make either one more effective for you?

WHAT'S MINE AND WHAT'S YOURS—EFFECTIVE BOUNDARIES

B oundary setting is a skill to essentially manage your environments. Since this section of the book is all about how the people, places, and things we interact with impact our ability to create successful changes, we need to be able to navigate all environments appropriately. The more skillful we become at boundary setting, the easier it will be to set clear intentions and actions in every environment.

Boundaries are the limits we set for acceptable behavior. They are intended to make relationships more mutually respectful and supportive. The absence of clear boundaries in any and all relationships (professional, romantic, friendship, etc.) can leave you feeling exhausted, both emotionally and physically, from guesswork, confusion, and constant adjustment to others' expectations. For more information on the health impact of poor boundaries, check out an article on the Livestrong website—*7 Ways to Set Clear Boundaries with People in Your Life*—that I contributed to.[72] When setting boundaries that really stick, one of the more challenging consequences is coming across as distant or cold. A couple of points on this:

1) such a perception may be a small price to pay for all the benefits;

2) the more practice you put into boundary setting, the better you will become at adjusting any outward signs of aloofness.

Since most of our time is spent at work, I want to elaborate on how to set effective boundaries in the workplace. However, you can practice setting effective boundaries across all your relationships and environments. Practicing good boundaries is a versatile skill. The more you do it in any one area, the better at it you will be in all domains of life.

Clear workplace boundaries positively affect you and your co-workers. Having clear boundaries helps to improve productivity, decrease stress, foster healthy relationships, and improve motivation. While boundary setting is largely determined by the particular relationship in question and the nature of the work involved, a 2012 study in *The Academy of Management Journal* found that evaluating and setting boundaries, had a positive effect on relationships in the workplace.[73] According to The University of California, San Francisco, when boundaries are clear, organizations are more efficient and groups are more productive.[74]

This research also applies to environments outside of the workplace. For instance, clear boundaries help to improve communication, clarity around responsibility, and expectations and can reduce the likelihood of conflict.

Often we learn the value of boundary setting through failure. If you have ever failed to speak up for yourself (I imagine this includes all of us), you'll relate to this next story.

My friend, Annie, once told me about a job she had right out of college that required her to manage a variety of accounts as well as pursue new ones. She was on the phone often, cold calling, pitching the company's services, doing follow-ups, etc. Her office was next to the owner's, and the walls were so thin that the owner could hear her conversations with clients and prospects. The instant she finished a call, the owner would fly into her office and nitpick her pitch. No detail was too small to critique.

He may have had some good points about how to be a better salesperson. But the invasion of privacy, her anxiety over when it would happen again, and his usual tone of irritation and disappointment didn't allow for any robust learning.

The failure on her part, as she described it, was that she didn't express herself. She did not explain to the owner that his communication was producing more nervousness and paranoia than anything else. In addition, she shared with me her regret that she didn't make an explicit request for the kind of leadership that would have helped her become a better employee. Had she and the owner come to an agreement about how to work together more effectively she would have learned a lot more about how to sell, prospect, and communicate with clients.

She didn't set the boundary because at the time she felt that it wasn't her place. Instead of tackling the discomfort directly, she put her head down and let the situation fester. Her major takeaway was that her failure to set proper boundaries didn't serve her, the owner, or the company at large.

~

I have witnessed the importance of clear boundary-setting as it relates to healthy living and sustainable positive change in a variety of circumstances.

Here are three very different examples of effective boundary setting:

- *I once worked with a small business that experienced challenges with employee turnover and couldn't identify the cause. When I delved into the nature of the conflict and the frustration, I discovered confusion concerning employee roles and responsibilities. I also discovered that not enough time had been allotted for employees to communicate their needs and concerns and share their successes with each other. A clearer understanding of expectations vastly improved the situation. In other words, better boundaries saved the day.*

- *When working as a therapist at a home for troubled youth, boundaries were always a major topic of discussion. Clearly establishing basic information—when our meetings would take place, where, for how long, what we would talk about, and if the clients had to participate or not—was imperative. Boundaries create safety. In this situation, clear boundaries also helped clients communicate more effectively. And clear communication contributed to the healing process in regard to psychological wounds.*

  This was a challenging environment to work in. The stories of abandonment, abuse, neglect, and violence were difficult to stomach. The only way to succeed in this environment was to set up certain boundaries. And it was tricky. I needed to show empathy, but not get wrapped up in taking personal responsibility for each person's healing. Determining the extent of our personal responsibility is a challenge, but vital to consider when evaluating boundaries.

- *I have seen clear boundaries create a safe space for communication in leadership teams as well. In one organization, we made a concerted effort to establish what was permissible to talk about during a leadership meeting. Team members found challenges in speaking up for themselves because there was confusion about what was reasonable and beneficial to discuss. After the group had a more transparent conversation about what they needed and built more trust among each other, they were able to make progress. They shifted into a more productive communication mode with each other and, ultimately, became a more dynamic and effective team. By building clear boundaries, they created success for themselves.*

"These examples are all well and good," you might say, *"but how do I put all of this into practice?"* Here are five strategies you can implement at work to set more effective boundaries. To make it easy to remember, just think of the first boundary infants come to know: CRIBS.

(C) **Cordial** – Setting clear boundaries does not require you to be dry, cold, or disconnected from your coworkers or others around you. In fact, quite the opposite, a friendly, positive attitude can impact your environment in a healthy way. Remember, one must strike a balance between setting a clear boundary and being approachable. How you choose to communicate will determine the effectiveness of the boundary.

(R) Responsibility – A clear idea of roles and responsibilities is crucial in a work environment. Any confusion over these matters necessitates communication with supervisors and co-workers to figure out who is responsible for which tasks. Creating an environment that encourages transparency and open dialogue will also encourage employees to speak up when they require further clarification about their responsibilities.

(I) Impersonal – It is important to understand the differences, obvious and subtle, between work relationships and personal relationships. You can foster a certain level of familiarity or closeness with your coworkers, but upholding a level of professionalism requires discernment. Over time, this can be challenging, especially in regard to our sensitivities or how we *"take things personally."* I certainly don't mean that we should be excusing bad behavior (racism, sexism, and/or otherwise blatantly offensive conduct). What I mean is that certain decisions in a work environment may be outside your control and may affect you unfavorably. There may be decisions made that don't make sense to you because you are not privy to all of the decision-making information. Also, remember that people's personalities, opinions, and preferences may be different than yours, which is OK. Our difference of opinion, as irritating as it may be at times, can be a major benefit (especially in terms of creating a more robust perspective). As in all your relationships, learning to not take things personally can be a game-changing perspective shift and a way to reduce stress and anxiety. This also touches on the strategy to build more empathy in that it demands that we rise above our own standpoint. (See more about building empathy in Section 2 – Heart.)

(B) Being the Leader – An environment without clear boundaries offers us an opportunity to step into a leadership role and exemplify how to set clear boundaries in regard to relationships and responsibilities. Regardless of your position, you have the choice to go with the flow or step up as a leader. Consider that you may have to carve out the leadership role you step into, especially if you can articulate the specific benefit it would add. For example, if you are on a sales team and you realize that there is a need for more frequent review of accounts, you may consider leading a weekly meeting in which strategies are discussed. Remember, your way of *"being"* creates a model for others. Always.

(S) Self-Care – Self-care may not seem like an obvious component of boundary setting. It is more of a preventative measure, but it is just as important as the other strategies. When you are run down, stressed out, irritable, or overwhelmed, boundaries tend to blur. Practicing self-care allows you not only to function at the highest level, but also to keep appropriate boundaries in clear sight.

CHAPTER 18 ACTIVITY

Let's put the five strategies listed above (CRIBS) into action. Even though these are strategies designed for work, they can be used all across your life domains. Embrace change by setting boundaries and track your success.

First, think of a challenge you've had and how setting a boundary would be advantageous. Then choose a boundary-setting strategy you want to practice. Note the dates you practice it and the associated life domain. Write down your observations when practicing this boundary-setting strategy. Explore boundary setting in multiple environments using different combinations. For instance, you can practice these strategies at work with family and friends and in your partnerships. More specifically, see this example below:

EXAMPLE

Challenge – *A co-worker has asked me to help him on his project. I agreed at first because I was flattered to be asked, but now I wonder if I'm being taken advantage of. I'm not sure if I'm technically responsible for this project and I haven't asked my boss because I don't want to ruffle any feathers. I need to resolve this because I have reached my capacity for workload and feel totally overwhelmed.*

Strategy	Responsibility
Dates	5/7/19
Life Domain	Work
Observations	After a 30-minute meeting discussing responsibility with my co-worker we determined that the project could be a shared venture and that if each of us focused on different aspects, it would save us both time.

List three examples for each of the five strategies (CRIBS).

Cordial

Responsibility

Impersonal

Being the Leader

Self-care

SPIRIT

"Why, sometimes I've believed as many as six impossible things before breakfast."

—*Lewis Carroll,*
Alice in Wonderland

Your beliefs directly affect your reality. In large part, your belief about the nature of human existence and your belief in what is possible within your life, define your experience. The tricky thing about belief is that it can lead to, or away from, creating the life experience we seek. Without oversight, our beliefs can cause damage and prevent us from creating what we want. They can also be wonderfully supportive and sustain us in the direst of circumstances. Either way, there is opportunity in examining our beliefs.

When we explore our beliefs we learn that we have more choices. There is value in exploring our belief in ourselves, in others, and the ever-present beliefs that we have inherited from our family and other environments. Our spiritual and religious beliefs, as well as beliefs in what is possible, often fall in line with what has preceded us (i.e. decisions made and opinions expressed by others). It's common to accept these beliefs without question. When we examine how our belief impacts us on a daily basis in all of our environments, we gain perspective. This examination may shake the foundation of what we hold on to so tightly. However, if we can shore up our courage and take the risk, there is true wisdom in exploring our beliefs: how they support us and how they may prevent us from optimizing our potential. This section takes us through the process of that examination.

19

DEALING WITH UNCERTAINTY

We live in an age of paradox. We understand more about the complexity of the universe around us and the intricacies of our internal world than ever before. Ironically, there is more discomfort with uncertainty today than at any other time in human history. In other words, while we have become more precise in our knowledge, we have also grown more fearful of being anything less than absolutely sure. And with that fear, comes indecision. Uncertainty we can't control. Indecision, fortunately, we can.

Constantly confronted with decisions in this modern world, we navigate a sea of distractions, a panorama of bright and shiny options, a mirage of endless possibility. Which restaurant to dine at, soap to use, exercise program to start, kind of insurance to get, partner to choose, etc.? The endless series of choices intended to liberate us can actually have the opposite effect: they often deprive us of time and attention we'd rather spend elsewhere.

Indecision and feeling overwhelmed go hand in hand. Feeling overwhelmed often compromises our judgment and our capacity to make positive changes in regard to career, relationship, or lifestyle. Just weighing which decision to make first can be exhausting.

So, how do we deal with uncertainty? And also, how do we manage indecision?

A friend and I were once talking about a new relationship she was in and the various aspects involved. We talked about her attraction to this new partner, the things they had in common, the fun they were having, etc. When the question of how, or if, to move forward came up, I asked what her motivation was to be with this person. She took a long time coming up with an answer. I got the impression that she was less sure about the relationship than she'd been letting on and that she appreciated the time to address her indecision. Obviously, we can feel connected to others—we can even fall in love—but what we ultimately want out of a relationship often takes time and some real thought to determine.

When we face the decision to continue a partnership or not, motivation is an important factor. In the context of relationships, motivation can come from a variety of sources, including desires for companionship, marriage, a family, good sex, and any combination of the above. The point is that motivation comes from somewhere, and I encourage you to seek it out in all your life domains to discover what is really driving your decisions. Deeply considering the motivation behind decisions leads to clarity.

Though understanding our motivations can help us deal with uncertainties and free ourselves from the ruts we find ourselves in from time to time, it doesn't mean that any kind of analysis is the be-all and end-all solution. Some degree of uncertainty is inevitable. We must make decisions even when we are less than 100 percent sure.

You may be asking yourself at this point, *"Why is this chapter in the section about spirituality?"* It's a fair question. I am exploring uncertainty here because when we are denied certainty, we must rely on faith in our decision-making.

I want to be clear about how I use the term, faith. For the purpose of this chapter I am using faith as a general term, not (necessarily) in its religious context, but as defined by our friends at Merriam-Webster: a *"firm belief in something for which there is no proof."*

Though I am choosing to apply a secular definition of faith, I am still going to tie it to spirituality. First, let's look at Merriam-Webster's definition of spirituality: *"The quality of being concerned with the human spirit or soul as opposed to material or physical things."*

This distinction between faith and spirituality is important. Spirituality offers a set of responses based, not on repeatable phenomena in the scientific sense, but on subjective experience and personal responses to questions such as, *Why are we here? Where do we go when we die? Is there a soul? What does it mean to be human?* These are open-ended questions, to which science and logic offer few clear-cut answers. Should you be so inclined to explore your own personal responses to these questions, I imagine that it will reveal the ways you rely on faith to deal with uncertainty.

Spirituality and faith highlight an important aspect of exploring change. Whether you are Christian, Jewish, Muslim, Buddhist, Hindu, Atheist, Agnostic, or identify in some other way, your affiliation has implications for how you behave, the choices you make, and how you see the world. Belief systems both support and test people's ability to make change. We are strongly tied to our version of the truth. Even in uncertain times or rather, *especially* in such times, how we make meaning of the world informs who we are. In other words, our belief systems define us as much as we define our belief systems.

So, when dealing with uncertainty, one option is to accept our lack of control and look instead to our belief system, whatever that may be.

There are other ways to handle uncertainty as well. Below, you'll find five strategies and ways to apply them.

FIVE TIPS TO MANAGE UNCERTAINTY

Learn to Follow Your Intuition – This may seem obvious, but there is power in understanding what your instincts tell you. An overabundance of options to choose among may distract you from applying your own wisdom. Practicing ways to reflect on your thoughts or feelings, such as journaling, art, mindfulness exercises, or some other daily practice may help you in this respect. See Chapter 5 for more resources on developing intuition.

Explore Your Assumptions, Values, and Self-Narratives – It's easy to get caught up analyzing a choice to death. Exploring your uncertainty from another angle may be helpful. Take a big step back and re-examine what you think is possible. This step back will offer you extra patience and equanimity when no *"right"* options jump out at you. For instance, if you are the kind of person who assumes that *"whenever I start something, I never finish it,"* explore how you can change that self-narrative. If you believe that *"making a lot of money is only for the greedy,"* examine how this assumption is serving your desire to be financially successful. For more guidance, ask yourself: *"How do my beliefs affect the way I handle uncertainty in this situation?"* If you assume that *"successful people are absolutely sure of themselves whenever they make big decisions,"* consider that everyone faces uncertainty in some way. You may rarely (if ever) be absolutely sure that you made the right decision, but a re-examination of the decision-making process will help you take new comfort in the face of uncertainty. You will be more likely to choose the more favorable path after re-evaluating which beliefs serve you best.

Consult an Unbiased Third Party – Speaking with an unbiased third party, such as a coach or therapist, can be an effective way to work through a decision. Someone who has little personal investment in your situation may be able to ask questions or offer insight in ways that those close to you cannot. Often, a unique question from an unbiased person helps us reexamine our own perspective and recalibrate our focus, which deepens our understanding of the situation.

Meditate – As we explored in Section 4 (Nourishment), meditation reduces stress and anxiety and even has a positive impact on us biologically.[75] Being present, or mindful, of our situation from moment to moment is another way to tap into our own understanding and make the best decision possible. Meditation may also offer a calming relief from discomfort, which often accompanies uncertainty.

Get Up and Move – The mind/body connection factors into everything we do, including our negotiations with uncertainties in life. Sometimes when we sit and try to think our way through every last option, when we strain to sift through all the pros and cons, it creates more confusion than clarity, especially when we don't take occasional breaks. Mental confusion creates physical stagnation, and vice-versa. Getting involved in regular exercise or simple movement may trigger a new way to look at a problem. Like an Etch a Sketch, movement can help to shake up our assumptions and reset our mind frame.

Some of the tips here are familiar; they come from other sections in the book. The important thing to remember about these seven principles (CHANGES) is that each influences, and is influenced by, the others. When we seek to create positive change, reduce stress, and improve our ability to adapt, we must consider our various life domains and how all are connected. As with the other sections, the intention here is to bring awareness to the intersection of the various life domains, not just to each alone. As we continue to explore the domain of Spirit, remember that it is connected to all the other domains and that addressing this network of connections is critical in creating the change you are after.

CHAPTER 19 ACTIVITY

First, identify a challenge you are uncertain about. Use the five tips in this chapter to actively work on reducing uncertainty or accepting it. Log your progress and note what insight you gained from applying each strategy.

Remember to mark the dates you practiced each strategy so you can compare frequency and effectiveness. This will help determine which work best for you.

EXAMPLE

Challenge - *While working with my team at work I am often in a state of stress and uncertainty which slows down the process and compromises our effectiveness and productivity.*

Strategy	Third party consult
Date Practiced	5/7/19
Insights	By working with a professional coach I have learned that I place too much emphasis on my work team's opinion when making a decision and that this dependency perpetuates my sense of uncertainty and stress.

20

SPIRITUALITY AND WELL-BEING

Interesting research about how spirituality and religion impact health and well-being has spurred lively debate. That said, this chapter is not a call for spiritual awakening or religious revival. I am not here to proselytize. We are all subject to our own particular beliefs, regardless of religious affiliation or lack thereof. This much is true. However, how you view your existence affects how you are able to create positive change. My recommendation is not to change what you believe, unless it's not serving you well. But I do recommend turning a critical eye to how your beliefs impact the other aspects of your life, such as how you think, make decisions, form relationships, build trust, manage stress, and conceive of what is possible for yourself and others.

Many people are raised with a certain belief system. They inherit it, incorporating it into their lives without question. If you haven't already, I say it's time to question it, regardless of what it is! Honestly evaluate how your beliefs impact your life. As you develop into the person you want to be, ask yourself tough questions to test what you truly believe. If you can step back from your beliefs, especially your long-held beliefs, and see them more objectively, you may be able to identify what is helping you and what is hurting you. This is especially important if your religious beliefs are near and dear to you. Have enough faith that your faith will stand up under close scrutiny.

When first meeting clients, I'm always curious about when the topic of religion or spirituality will first come up. I am fascinated by belief systems and especially intrigued by the similarities among them. It's bizarre to me that such heated conflict can flare up over what I see as the interpretation of language. The philosophies may be strikingly similar, but when articulation of those philosophies differs, discontent, disagreement, or even violence erupts. We humans can be rather nitpicky creatures, can't we? I think such conflicts also speak to the supreme importance of how we communicate.

The discourses of Jesus, the teachings of Buddha, and the Talmud all express very similar lessons regarding compassion and respect for others. Granted, the words each uses vary, but the concepts overlap. Basic tenets of peace and nonviolence crop up all throughout the Bible, the Koran, the Bhagavad-Gita, and other holy texts. There are endless examples of similarities across belief systems.

When I meet with new clients, belief systems can be a sticky issue. For example, I once met with a potential client to discuss working together in a coaching capacity and things seemed to be going very well. Let's call this client Mary. Mary was interested in exploring how to reduce stress, set boundaries to strike a healthier work/life balance, and institute better practices as a leader in her small business. Mary and I connected on our shared philosophies concerning how to create change and effective leadership. We also shared an interest in the close relationship between personal and professional development. She wanted to incorporate spirituality into our work. I usually welcome such a request because I have seen the forward momentum that religious beliefs add to people's lives. So, I was happy to incorporate her faith into our dialogue.

After agreeing that we could incorporate spirituality into our work together, Mary started to ask questions about my belief system. Now, thus far in our conversation we had found that our values aligned in regard to how to treat clients/customers, ways of engaging with employees, and other ethical aspects of effective business leadership. Both of us had identified doing work with purpose and passion and being of service to others as high priorities. Plus, we shared interests in some of the same thought-leaders in nutrition as well as a love for martial arts. We had made some real connections.

When I shared my summation of our connection and alignment, I encountered a catch. My attempt at a diplomatic response about our connection and value-alignment suggesting promising results didn't exactly answer the question, and Mary noticed. She pressed me on the issue: were we of the same religious affiliation. We explored why this was important to her and how this may impact our work. The fact that we did not share the same religious beliefs became an impasse for us. We did not end up working together.

Unfortunately, religious differences are a common barrier to human connection. When we don't find common identification, when we don't ascribe to the same religious language, we often run into a stalemate. I understand that people want to find commonality with others, and therefore seek out those who share their belief system. I simply believe that people would also benefit by taking the opportunity to explore what is behind the language they use to describe their belief system. What if we could explore our common ground before letting our different use of labels create barriers between us?

Intergroup conflict aside, there is plenty of evidence to support the notion that belief systems can be helpful to us in ways that go beyond the spiritual. For example, an article from *The Journal of Behavioral Medicine* states, *"Spirituality, as defined as the combination of existential and religious well-being, is related to both emotional well-being and quality of life."*[76]

According to *The Journal of Health Psychology*, research shows that religious coping methods have an impact on health. The journal cited a study that demonstrated *"Positive methods of religious coping (e.g., seeking spiritual support, benevolent religious reappraisals) were associated with improvements in health and negative methods of religious coping (e.g., punishing God reappraisal, interpersonal religious discontent) were predictive of declines in health."*[77]

If those terms in parentheses gave you pause, you're not alone. Let's clarify. When religious believers felt reassured of divine love or attributed a positive turn of events to the blessings of a higher power, they experienced better physical health. By contrast, when people dealt with tense relationships in a religious context or attributed misfortunes to divine punishment, they experienced worse physical health.

When people shift their focus or modify their beliefs, they can create changes. As evidenced by *The Journal of Health Psychology* study, focusing on negative often tends to lead to negative outcomes and focusing on positive tends to lead to positive outcomes. Therefore, exploring our beliefs is a vital component of creating effective change. That said, even if switching your perspective from negative to positive were as easy as flipping a light (to be clear, it's not), it alone wouldn't be enough to create the changes you seek. Additional steps and resources are required. As you've read so far in this book, I advocate a holistic approach. An effective perspective-shift will pertain to Spirit and Cognition and will inspire Action toward meaningful CHANGES. The seven dimensions in this book and their interaction offer us lenses to examine what is holding us back and what needs to be developed.

Note: This is not a book about creating your reality by thinking happy thoughts.

Belief and well-being are connected, but they are just two of the factors that influence our ability to create change.

Still need some evidence? How about this: according to a meta-analysis of 49 studies exploring the relationship between religious coping methods and psychological adjustment to stress, it was found that positive and negative coping are related to positive and negative adjustment to stress, respectively.[78]

Well-being and belief systems are not limited to one's personal life, though. There is also evidence to show that spirituality impacts the organization. According to a 2016 article in *The International Journal of Indian Psychology*, spirituality in the workplace is related to inspired leadership, a strong organizational base, organizational integrity, a positive work environment, and a sense of community among members, among other positive qualities.[79]

According to a 2012 study in the journal, *Personality and Individual Differences*, a correlation was found between spirituality and positive outcomes except when workplace aggression was present. In the presence of workplace aggression, spiritual employees tended to be more vulnerable to negative outcomes than less spiritual employees.[80]

Having seen how belief systems impact us both personally and professionally, we have come to the point to take action. Challenging your beliefs may bring up some fundamental questions, fears, judgments, and insecurities. Remember, if you feel you need additional support, consider calling a coach or therapist to help you work through the process.

CHAPTER 20 ACTIVITY

Jot down a specific change you have been trying to make. Now journal on the following questions:

- *What does your belief system tell you about what you are capable of changing in your life?*
- *What do you know about other belief systems available?*
- *Who can you reach out to as a resource for understanding more about your belief system or alternatives?*

If you are unsure how to describe your belief system, that's okay. Consider asking three people who know you well to describe what they think you believe in. Would they describe you as religious, spiritual, agnostic, atheist, or something else? Ask them to give you feedback on the following three questions:

1) How do you see my belief system supporting me or holding me back?

2) What do you think is most important to me when it comes to religion/spirituality?

3) How have you seen me express my spiritual/religious beliefs? Can you give specific examples?

Now that you have some feedback, you can decide what to do with it. Consider the following questions:

- *From the questions you answered yourself and the feedback you received, do any themes emerge?? If so, what insights do they provide?*
- *What actions can you commit to taking based on the insights you have gathered?*

BELIEF AND REALITY

I once worked with a man who was certain that aliens have graced us with their presence, are still here in some fashion, and will resurface at some point. For the purposes of this story, let's call him James.

James had been diagnosed with a mental health disorder that had troubled him for much of his life. His grasp of reality was different than mine or that of most folks I knew. He could go on and on about aliens, his theories about how they had made contact, the evidence that guaranteed their return, and his own experiences with them. The curious thing about these stories was how convincing they were. James was a sweet, engaging man. His stories may have been fantastic, but they gave me an insight into his reality.

James and I would usually spend our time together outside. When James was surrounded by nature, he always struck me as the most calm and peaceful version of himself. Occasionally, we would venture into town. While in town, James enjoyed going to thrift shops, music stores (he had excellent taste in music), and other arts and crafts dealers in search of fun collectibles he could take back to his tiny home in the woods.

For James, the joy of browsing the shops was almost worth the discomfort of being among others. People could be a trigger. He'd obsess over any *perceived* insult. Operative word: perceived.

When we were together, I wouldn't even notice the same thing that would irritate him to no end.

During our time together, we set a variety of goals. He wanted to incorporate coping methods to manage his negative reactions, increase his ability to function independently, and reduce his paranoia/delusions. Often, James made progress. Sometimes, he struggled significantly. During the times that he did well, he was able to integrate the various aspects of his life. By doing so, he deepened his understanding of his paranoia, became more aware of the support available to him, embraced his version of faith, took care of himself physically, and connected with the people he loved.

James may not remind you of anyone you have encountered. Thankfully, most of us don't have to wrestle with what is real and what is delusion, at least, not on a regular basis. But James's ability to create change is quite similar to ours.

James's courage to take stock of his life and transform it is an inspiration to me. Evaluating our version of the truth and questioning its validity is both courageous and liberating. Exploring our reality will help us distill what we truly believe in. It will also highlight our responses to grand philosophical questions, such as *Why am I here?* and *Where am I headed?*

Perhaps even more pertinent are these two questions:

1) How does your outlook or your idea of what is possible serve you or sabotage you?

2) What are you willing to do to challenge this mode of perception?

In the scientific journal, *Current Biology*, a 2013 study presents evidence of how our imagination can actually affect our senses.

For example, imagining a sound can alter what we report having seen, and imagining visual stimuli can impact what we think we hear.[81]

There may be more to the phrase *"your mind is playing tricks on you"* than we think. There is much more evidence to show that our perception can influence us in surprising ways.

Copious data support the idea that self-efficacy (belief in one's self) contributes to good health.[82] You may read this and think, *"Well of course, if someone believes in themselves, then they'll spend more time taking care of themselves."* True, but belief and reality are even more tightly connected.

For example, there is evidence to show that our personality can affect our perception. A 2017 article in *The Journal of Research in Personality* cites evidence that people who are more open to new experiences tend to possess greater powers of visual perception.[83] To clarify, the study referenced here goes beyond saying that people who are more open-minded also tend to be more observant. It proposes that more open-minded subjects showed higher visual function on the most basic level before the brain even recognizes objects. In short, a person who has a more open, flexible personality may actually see and observe more of what is physically in front of them.

There's more. In another study, we see more evidence for how a belief impacts our biology. Psychology Professor Dr. Segerstrom at the University of Kentucky conducted a study and concluded that as optimistic expectancies increased, so did cell-mediated immunity.[84] In other words, when subjects assumed a more optimistic outlook, they experienced an immunity boost.

Of course, there are many studies that suggest that a subject's physical reality changes due to a shift in thinking. For instance, the placebo effect (a psychological phenomenon in which a substance or intervention that has no scientifically proven therapeutic effect actually leads to improvement). Not to go too far down the rabbit hole, but let me share one quick placebo study that I think is particularly fascinating.

[A side note for all you skeptics out there: data on perception, placebo, body/mind connectivity, and the like are constantly evolving.]

Though follow-up research is still needed, there are interesting findings that link the placebo effect to a reduction of pain and anxiety. There is even documented evidence of the placebo effect improving symptoms related to Parkinson's disease and aiding in certain surgical procedures.[85]

Let me save you some time and effort before you go poring over the studies I present or searching for some of your own to refute these claims. Whether or not you believe that a belief can change an outcome, I invite you to experiment for yourself. Often we become so enmeshed in our habits and ways of being that we can lose track of how these patterns affect us.

The opportunity for experimenting with new beliefs, new expectations, and new possibilities is always there. It is an open-ended invitation waiting for your mindful response.

What is real? What is possible? What can be created? You alone need to answer these critical questions in the precious time you have here. Don't wait.

CHAPTER 21 ACTIVITY

Taking actions that challenge your current perceptions can be an effective way to initiate a change process or re-energize one that has run out of steam. The following exercise may reorient you on your journey toward effective changemaking. Answer the following questions:

- *What strong beliefs underpin your perceived reality?*
- *What is an alternative way to consider these beliefs? For instance, if you believe that homeless people probably came by their current situation because they didn't work hard enough, what is an alternative position on this?*
- *What is a belief you inherited as a child that you have never challenged?*
- *If you were to challenge this belief, what questions would you ask, or how would you challenge it?*
- *What is one belief you have that works against you in creating the life you want?*
- *What are you willing to do to let go of this belief?*
- *What are three actions you will commit to taking to eliminate this detrimental belief? After you complete each commitment, take note of your observations and insights.*

CHANGES IN MOTION

WHERE DO YOU SEE YOURSELF IN FIVE YEARS?

I f you've avoided the exercises in the book, creating five-year goals can be a great place to start. Depending on where you started reading, this chapter can serve either as closure or as an introduction to CHANGES.

As you consider what you want to change about your professional or personal life, you now have a strategy to employ. Assessing the seven principles in CHANGES will help you identify which areas in your life are not getting enough attention as well as which areas are thriving. In this chapter we'll explore how to use these seven principles to build your ability to adapt, accomplish goals, and do so without major stress. Specifically, we'll explore the seven principles through the frame of creating a five-year plan.

In considering where you'll be in five years, you must first evaluate what you truly want. You can use the CHANGES tool to determine what you would like to see differently across the various areas in your life.

For our purposes here, I would recommend focusing on what you'd like to accomplish over a five-year period. As you do this, you might consider asking yourself the following questions:

- *How do I want to be thinking differently? (Cognition)*

223

- How might I be more emotionally available and resilient, and what emotional reactions will I better manage? (Heart)
- What behaviors or practices will be totally different in five years? (Action)
- How will I be taking care of my body in a way that I have never done before? (Nourishment)
- What kinds of positive risks will I be taking that I won't allow myself to take today? (Guts)
- How will the friends, community, activities or work I am engaged in be different? (Environment)
- What beliefs might I challenge over the course of the next five years, and what will I choose to believe that is very different than what I currently believe? (Spirit)

Another way to think about what you want in your life is to create a vision board. It's a fun, creative way to explore what you truly desire for yourself. Though there are a bunch of ways to make a vision board, in essence, you take a sheet of poster board and fill it with pictures (photographs, drawings, images cut out from print media, etc.), phrases, and symbols that represent your aspirations. For a deeper dive I recommend Jack Canfield's approach.[86]

Let's be clear here. Creating a board full of all the things you want and ways you want to be is a fun exercise, but should not be confused with all the rest of the hard work required in reaching your goals. In my experience, the process of creating a vision board offers three major benefits.

1) It compels you to ask yourself what you truly want in your life.

2) It demands that you find visual representation for those desires. Do not discount the importance of this part. Any expression of a desire helps you to communicate it to others and define what it is for yourself. (During the process, you may discover that your sense of what you truly want undergoes changes.)

3) When finished, the board acts as a visual reminder of what you *"say"* you want. It also functions as a tool for accountability. It should elicit the question, *"What am I doing* **right now** *to attain these goals?"*

As you well know by now, you realize that achieving what you want is not just about setting intention and wishing your way through change. While visualization is important, you must combine it with all the other principles in this book.

Unless we establish strong intentions, we are letting someone else lead. Either we set our own direction or we allow our direction to be set for us. The exercise of exploring where you'll be in five years puts you in charge.

Expressing your goals increases the likelihood of attaining them. According to a study by Psychology Professor Dr. Gail Matthews, 70 percent of participants who shared their goals achieved them.[87] In other words, the odds are in your favor if you commit a goal to paper or tell someone about it.

Of course, there is a lot of distraction around us, begging for our attention. Distractions steal our time and energy from seeking the goals we are after. By using the various strategies in the seven dimensions we discuss in this book, we can help reduce distraction.

Having a plan in place for what you want should include all the steps clearly designated along the way. Here are some tips for making a five-year plan that will help you ensure success.

FIVE TIPS FOR CREATING A FIVE-YEAR PLAN

MORE THAN A FIVE-YEAR PLAN

Creating a five-year plan is more than answering the question, *"Where will I be in five years?"* It's about establishing new patterns of intention, so that you know more about what you want, where you're headed, and how you'll get there. It's about self-discovery. It's about setting a trajectory for long-lasting change that leads to success. When envisioning how your upcoming years will unfold, consider that this visualization process (similar to creating the vision board) may be just as valuable as the goals you are setting. By outlining your goals and intentions you will also be practicing a new way of thinking and perhaps even establishing new beliefs for what is possible, which incorporates two of the seven principles in this book, Cognition and Spirit.

WHERE WERE YOU FIVE YEARS AGO?

Considering where you came from and how you got to where you are—however you want to interpret those questions—will help you identify your patterns of behavior. Most likely, these patterns have affected your goals and aspirations in ways both positive and negative. Alternatively, you may learn that you have not been adequately intentional about where you were going. Skip the self-shaming and start exploring how to create more self-direction.

WHAT ARE YOU WILLING TO GIVE UP?

Setting an intention for self-development or improvement in some area in your life may involve sacrifice. We only have so much time every day, and setting priorities for what we want often requires letting go or replacing. A great way to evaluate what you may need to give up is to regularly ask yourself,

"How is what I'm doing right now getting me closer to where I want to be in five years, and if it isn't, what am I willing to sacrifice?"

HOW SELF-DISCIPLINED ARE YOU AND HOW CAN THIS IMPROVE?

This examination is related to the previous one. Any sort of change takes a certain level of discipline. If you decide your self-discipline needs improvement, then exploring ways to practice is helpful, if not necessary. Discipline can be developed in many ways. (Refer back to Chapter 14 on self-discipline, if you've skipped ahead.)

LET GO OF LIMITING BELIEFS

Exploring which of your beliefs serve you well, and which ones don't, will help to not only develop your five-year plan, but also to carry it out. Fear often gets in the way of exploring goals by convincing you that you may not be able or ready to achieve them. Reducing fear and limiting beliefs will allow you to recognize and contemplate available options and set more realistic goals. (See Chapter 13 and all of Section 7 for more details on letting go of limiting beliefs.)

CHANGES IN MOTION ACTIVITY

This activity will use the questions above, but in a different order. Follow the steps to get the most out of this activity.

Step One – Answer some (or all) of the questions below before writing out your five-year plan.

» *Where were you five years ago? What were you doing, how were you feeling, and what did you want?*

» *What are you willing to sacrifice to get what you want?*

» *What can you give up now, so that you'll have more time/ money/energy to get what you truly want later?*

» *What current patterns and habits can you work on modifying to increase the likelihood of success?*

» *How can you improve your self-discipline? Think of a time when you felt satisfied with the discipline in your life. What did you start, stop, or do more of to institute this level of discipline.*

» *What limiting beliefs do you need to let go of? Do any of your beliefs, currently or historically, get in the way of your success? Which ones?*

» *What patterns or behaviors do you want to create or eliminate?*

» *In five years, how you want to be thinking differently?*

» *In five years, how will you be more emotionally available and resilient, and what emotional reactions will you better manage?*

» *What behaviors or practices will be totally different in five years?*

» *How will you be taking care of your body in a way that you have never done before?*

» *What kinds of positive risks will you be taking in five years that you won't allow yourself to take today?*

» *How will the friends, community, activities or work you are engaged in be different in five years?*

» *What beliefs might you challenge over the course of the next five years, and what will you choose to believe that is very different than what you currently believe?*

Step Two – Use the insight you gained from answering the questions as a springboard for creating your plan. Don't skimp when answering the questions. Include specific details to create a clear vision for yourself.

Step Three – Finally, write a few achievable goals to help start you on your path.

Now, what is your five-year plan? Write it out and then write out your first three goals.

PART TWO

HOW TO FIND THE RIGHT HELPING PROFESSIONAL

This section of the book is not connected to the self-initiated work of Part One. It is not about the CHANGES model, although some questions in Part Two may sound a bit familiar.

I hope that by going through the exercises in Part One, you've made strides toward achieving the positive change you were seeking. If you are still feeling you're not quite all the way there, no problem. Sometimes, additional assistance is needed. Believe me, I get it. And so, this personal development book will now pivot to address that concern.

As I've said, this book is about understanding the various aspects of ourselves and how they influence our success and failure. Still, even with the best of intentions and most vigilant work on all the right things, it's extremely helpful to have third-party support. We are going to unpack that process a bit.

Some of the most common questions I've received over the course of my career as a professional coach, consultant, and therapist, include variations of the following:

How do I find the right coach or therapist?

*What's the difference between coaching,
therapy and other helping professions?*

*How do I know which one to hire? A coach,
or a therapist, or someone else?*

In the pages ahead we'll answer all three questions and you will be prepared to choose, hire, and work with the right helping professional... should you want to. Remember, if you need help, that's ok. The complexity of our life experience often requires assistance to untangle. This complexity is a beautiful paradox: in its specificity, it makes us unique, but in general, it connects us to each other.

THERAPY - SEPARATING FACT FROM FICTION

What is therapy, anyway? Why would anyone pay money just to sit and talk to someone else? Why not just talk out my problems with a friend, co-worker, or family member and save all that money?

've heard all these questions and more. And yet, therapy is estimated to be a $15 billion per year industry.[88]

A little FYI before we get started: the term, behavioral health, is often interchanged with *"mental health"* and the term, therapy, is also often interchanged with *"psychotherapy"* and *"counseling."* These terms are not meant to be limited to those who struggle with a disorder. From time to time, we all run into challenges such as depression, anxiety, stress, anger, etc. This is normal. There are also diagnoses for some of these challenges if they meet certain criteria. But I don't want to bore you with the details. Think of it this way, mental health and behavioral health are umbrella terms to cover services, which help people cope with, resolve, or manage challenges regarding emotional, mental, or behavioral issues.

We all experience various levels of functioning on any given day. We refer to these emotional, physical, and behavioral fluctuations as health. Sometimes we present strong, healthy versions of ourselves, and sometimes we present weak, sickly versions. Even if we do accurately identify what is going on within us, we may lack the training, skills, and wherewithal to understand and manage these variations in our health. This is where therapy can be truly beneficial.

When seeking a therapist, narrow your search by considering your objective. Keep in mind that within the field of therapy, there are different concentrations. Most states require that anyone seeking to become a licensed therapist first obtain a master's degree in one of four disciplines.

Psychology – The American Psychological Association defines Psychology as *"the study of the mind and behavior. The discipline embraces all aspects of the human experience— from the functions of the brain to the actions of nations, from child development to care for the aged. In every conceivable setting from scientific research centers to mental healthcare services, the understanding of behavior is the enterprise of psychologists."*[89]

Social work – The National Association of Social Work defines social work practice as *"the professional application of social work values, principles, and techniques to one or more of the following ends: helping people obtain tangible services; counseling and psychotherapy with individuals, families, and groups; helping communities or groups provide or improve* social and health services; and participating in legislative processes."[90]

Marriage and family therapy – The American Association of Marriage and Family Therapy defines marriage and family therapy in the following way, *"A family's patterns of behavior influences the individual and therefore may need to be a part of the treatment plan. In marriage and family therapy, the unit of treatment isn't just the person—even if only a single person is interviewed —it is the set of relationships in which the person is imbedded."*[91]

Counseling – The American Counseling Association defines counseling as *"a professional relationship that empowers diverse individuals, families, and groups to accomplish mental health, wellness, education, and career goals."*[92]

The field of Psychiatry is related to the four disciplines above, but it requires a medical degree.

Psychiatry – Psychiatrists sometimes practice as therapists. The main difference between Psychiatry and the others is that a psychiatrist can prescribe medication. Also, the definition by the American Psychiatric Association states that *"Psychiatry is the branch of medicine focused on the diagnosis, treatment and prevention of mental, emotional and behavioral disorders. A psychiatrist is a medical doctor (an M.D. or D.O.) who specializes in mental health, including substance use disorders. Psychiatrists are qualified to assess both the mental and physical aspects of psychological problems."*[93]

When seeking a psychiatrist, you may also encounter the term, **Psychiatric Mental Health Nurse Practitioner.**

The American Psychiatric Nurses Association states that Psychiatric Mental Health Nurse Practitioners *"apply the nursing process to assess, diagnose, and treat individuals and families with psychiatric disorders or the potential for such disorders using their full scope of therapeutic skills, including the prescription of medication and administration of psychotherapy."*[94]

Granted, there is a lot of overlap among these descriptions. There are differences among these disciplines, but when it comes to finding a therapist, I believe they are mere technicalities and that what matters far more are the particular qualities of the person in front of you.

For the purposes of this book, I will add to the mix the term, coaching, which I'll be discussing more in the following chapters. For now, I'll make the basic distinction that counseling/therapy is about resolving pain, while coaching is about developing or improving a characteristic.

To lay the groundwork of understanding, we should look at the different options within behavioral health. Approaches and styles vary widely.

Before we dive into some of the specializations within therapy, a small note about the process. If all you know about therapy comes from TV and the movies, allow me to dispel some myths. While styles vary, each therapy session consists of a conversation between client and therapist about what is working well and what is causing pain in the client's life. The depth, the emphasis on history or on the future, and the kinds of questions discussed, will vary, depending on the therapist.

Therapists can specialize in different areas, including, but not limited to:

- *Couples therapy*
- *Child therapy*
- *Sex therapy*
- *Trauma therapy*
- *Family therapy*
- *Substance abuse therapy*

While the subject matter differs among these specializations, the basic therapeutic framework is similar. In the pages to come, we'll explore how to sift through all the options of finding a therapist.

WHERE TO FIND A THERAPIST

Here are a few tips on where to start your search for a therapist in terms of location and other considerations. The behavioral health specialists working at these venues may be credentialed in any one of the disciplines mentioned previously.

All of the options you'll find in the coming pages have advantages and drawbacks. By exploring these resources, you'll develop a good sense of which option is the most appropriate for you.

SCHOOLS

There are usually therapeutic resources available to students at all levels of education, ranging from grade school and high school counselors to therapists at universities. If you are searching for therapy as a student or for a student, it is likely that, at the very least, the school will offer you a referral to a local therapist based on the concern you have. At the collegiate level, you may access therapy services directly, usually right there on campus. Many universities have robust departments dedicated to serving the mental health needs of students and staff. Resources will largely depend on the particular educational institution.

COMMUNITY MENTAL HEALTH

Most communities have access to some kind social service program. These places are referred to as community mental health centers, which are great resources for a variety of reasons.

For new therapists just out of graduate school and seeking career experience, community mental health centers are a common starting point. This does not mean that such venues are operated exclusively by inexperienced therapists doing residency programs. I worked in the community mental health system for years and found nearly all of my colleagues to be educated, insightful, and compassionate therapists. There are a variety of advantages to working with someone in this environment, including the fact that these programs often accept all kinds of insurance. If you don't have insurance, community mental health centers often allow clients to pay for services at a reduced rate. There are even some grant-funded programs that offer free services. Such financial matters are dependent upon the funding and availability in your state and local community.

Of course, there are also a few drawbacks to community health centers. The environment is not as personalized, the practitioners are often overworked and stressed, and you may experience longer wait times.

PRIVATE PRACTICE & GROUP PRACTICE

There are many advantages to working with a therapist in private practice. Private practice therapy offers independence and flexibility. For the client, private practice therapists allow out-of-pocket (private) payment, which eliminates the necessity for a specific diagnosis or a billing submission to insurance companies—a definite plus for many people. More about the complexities of mental health diagnosis and insurance in the coming pages.

Group practices offer the same flexibility and independence as individual private practice, but with additional support. In certain cases, group practices offer options to see practitioners who offer complimentary therapeutic services. For instance, topics such as nutrition, fitness, and alternative medicine are sometimes integrated in group practices. Group or private practice environments are also usually designed to be less institutional and more casual.

EMPLOYEE ASSISTANCE PROGRAM

Employee Assistance Programs (EAPs) are benefits offered to employees that are either a component of a medical plan or offered as an additional employee benefit outside of the medical plan. Yes, some companies sponsor therapy services for their employees.

During my time in the EAP industry I was surprised that so many of the employees were unaware of the services available to them. EAPs allow employees to seek counseling services free of charge within certain criteria. To see if your organization has an EAP, contact your human resources department. Larger organizations are more likely to offer EAPs. This excellent resource may provide free services; if nothing else, it will support you in your search for the right service.

VETERANS ADMINISTRATION

Veterans Administration (VA) locations have become hubs for therapy because of recent demands for the services of social workers, psychologists, psychiatrists, and counselors. Behavioral health specialists working in the VA deal with a wide range of issues, including Post Traumatic Stress Disorder (PTSD), addictions, trauma, and family-dynamics issues. Thanks to the recent expansion of mental health services within the VA system, there are now many more resources available for veterans.

HOSPITAL

Mental health services in a hospital encompass an array of roles, depending on the needs of each patient and family. There is evidence to show that hospitals are becoming more popular settings for mental health workers.[95] Experts attribute this to healthcare transitioning to an integrated care model.[96] For those of you seeking mental health services, this is good news as it broadens your range of options.

CRISIS INTERVENTIONIST

The role of a crisis interventionist may vary depending on context, but it usually involves helping individuals or organizations debrief from a specific crisis and providing them with necessary resources and support. Crisis workers are often brought into hospitals to intervene when someone is in need of emergency therapeutic services. Crisis workers also provide *"safety checks"* in the community, such as when someone poses the risk of harming him/herself or others. When called in, crisis interventionists explore other immediate resources for clients and in extreme cases, recommend involuntary psychiatric hospitalization. In addition, most hospitals will either have internal services or a contract with agencies that can provide help for those in need 24 hours a day. To learn more about crisis intervention, contact your local community health agency or, in an emergency, dial 911.

CORRECTIONAL FACILITY

I add this section to emphasize the importance of rehabilitation. The right kind of mental health services can impact sustainable change, no matter the context. According to an article in the journal, *Law and Human Behavior*, mental health intervention has proven effective in reducing recidivism.[97] According to a 2014 article in *The American Journal of Public Health*, 26 percent of almost 20,000 inmates surveyed had been diagnosed with a mental health condition in their lifetime. In addition, more than 50 percent of inmates in this study were not receiving the medication they needed upon entry to prison.[98] Thankfully, according to a 2017 article in the journal, *World Psychiatry*, there is an emergence of treatment approaches within prisons and within the legal system as a whole.[99] And as these types of therapeutic services expand, we see more and more benefits.

SOME OBSERVATIONS AND REASSURANCE

When searching for a helping professional, there are a few other roadblocks you may come across. In the following pages, we'll explore some common complaints, pushbacks, and irritations I've encountered from clients, colleagues, friends and family about the field of therapy over the years.

THE COMPLEXITIES OF THE MENTAL HEALTH SYSTEM

The mental health system in the US is currently in flux. What is status quo today (2019) will most likely undergo a host of changes, most of which we cannot predict. That said, I believe the general issues I address below will still be relevant for the foreseeable future and therefore will require navigation.

One of the major complexities that we should address is the issue of diagnosis, which (perhaps surprisingly) is related to payment. The term, diagnosis, may need a little technical explanation. Mental health diagnostic criteria come from an industry tool called the Diagnostic Statistical Manual (DSM) that presents agreed-upon criteria and standards for every mental health diagnosis. When seeking therapy, people often want to use their insurance to pay for it. This is perfectly understand-able. Insurance coverage comes with a small catch, however. In order for insurance companies to cover treatment, they need to see a diagnosis from the therapist.

Now why is this complicated? Because mental health and medical health norms/practices are always changing, we can't be sure (at least, not for long) how or if prior conditions will be an issue for the consumer in the future. To clarify, prior conditions are diagnoses (it could be anything, but depression or anxiety are two of the most common) that stay on an individual's med-ical record. The risk involves who may access such information (future employers, volunteer organizations, military, licensure boards, school, etc.) as well as what they might do with said in-formation. For instance, we can envision a scenario in which an employer chooses not to hire based solely on prior conditions, regardless of excellent qualifications.

For example, a survey of medical doctors from all 50 states revealed that over half of them believed they themselves may meet DSM criteria for a mental health diagnosis but avoided seeking treatment for fear of it being reported to their medical board.[100]

So you may be thinking, *"Well, if doctors meet criteria for a mental health diagnosis, shouldn't their board know about it and do something?"* To which I would answer, *"Maybe."* I'll explain with the following example, an amalgam of scenarios I personally witnessed as a therapist.

Chad, a middle-aged doctor, was going through a divorce. He'd been in love with his wife for 20 years and they had two wonderful children. The separation sent Chad into a deep sad-ness. As a result, he struggled with his work, his friendships, and his efforts to redefine his post-divorce identity as a father, partner, etc. Chad's transition was tough, but not unlike that of anyone else going through a similar life loss. He decided to seek therapy for emotional support and to learn ways to cope with his hardship. Based on his initial interview and his preference to use his insurance, the therapist diagnosed him with depression. To be clear, the therapist had reviewed the DSM's definition of depression and had confirmed that Chad met the criteria. Over a period of six months or so, Chad made great progress in therapy, continued to adjust to his new circumstance, and closed out his meetings with his therapist. Subsequently, Chad no longer met the criteria for depression, but his diagnosis stayed with him.

The complexities here are vast. Would it have been better for Chad if the therapist had not given him the diagnosis? Does Chad actually have a biological predisposition to clinical depression? Is Chad just a normal guy, who, in dealing with life-altering circumstances, needed some temporary support? Would it be fair that Chad's diagnosis stay on his record like a blemish throughout his professional career, potentially precluding future opportunities? Is it reasonable to assume a therapist can accurately understand someone's experience enough to offer a diagnosis after just one meeting with them? Some of these questions surely require a deeper understanding of the clinical nuances of depression, but I think you probably get my point: these issues are not easily resolved and can lead to real distress. Needless to say, the mental health and medical health systems could use an overhaul.

As a would-be consumer, you should know the complications of the mental health system before you enter it. I encourage you to discuss the issue of diagnosis with any therapist with whom you consider working.

BUSTING THE MYTH THAT THERAPY SUCKS

The stigma around seeking help or guidance is a somewhat unusual cultural phenomenon. It is certainly influenced by gender, geography, cultural background, and socioeconomic class. It should come as no surprise that promoting therapy as a cultural norm and reducing the stigma around it increases the numbers of those who seek it out.[101] I hope the following examples from my own career will help you overcome any reservations you may have about seeking help.

THROWING THE BABY OUT WITH THE BATHWATER

You may have heard some version of the old complaint, *"I tried therapy once and didn't like it."* As is the case with any social interaction (dating or friendship, for instance), the particular connection you have with your therapist is a crucial factor to consider. Research shows that the right fit with a helping professional is one of the best predictors of positive change.[102]

It may take some time and effort to find a therapist you connect with. Unfortunately, it often happens that when clients don't connect with a new therapist, they quit and then chalk up their experience to the general ineffectiveness of all therapy. I believe that for the sake of finding the right fit, clients should take advantage of the opportunity to analyze what didn't work with their interactions. A poor connection may be due to several factors, including differences in communication style, cultural differences, or generational differences. It may be that the therapist pushes the client too hard (or not hard enough), or that the client does not understand the importance of connection as a key to success. Clients may also mistakenly assume that the therapist has some kind of cure-all wisdom to unveil to them. In such circumstances clients may ignore their own intuition, which is usually a mistake. It is the therapist's job to enable the client's own wisdom to come forward, not to tell the client how to live.

Therapists are like any other professional: there are great ones, good ones, and some who shouldn't be in the field at all. To give you perspective, imagine that a plumber you hire does a bad job. Would you discount the profession of plumbing altogether or simply call a different plumber? Therapy is no different. If you have a negative experience, don't give up. Don't assume the process sucks just because it didn't work out the first time. There is likely to be a therapist out there who is right for you. At the end of this chapter I've added tools intended to expedite this discovery process.

"THERAPY DOESN'T WORK"

When clients assume that therapy is wasting their time because after a handful of sessions they haven't seen the immediate results they were expecting, they fail to consider the element of time. Changing behavior, perspective, or habits sometimes takes time. And patience. Going to a few therapy sessions and quitting after not seeing immediate results is like working out a few times, failing to lose twenty pounds, and giving up.

Clients should know how to get the most out of working with a therapist. Having a discussion early in the therapy process about what you hope to gain and should expect from the experience is critical for optimal results. Thankfully, many therapists do start this way. But don't be afraid to ask questions if you find yourself in a situation in which the process is not perfectly clear.

It is also important to understand the basic parameters of a therapy session. Each time you meet with a therapist, it is typically for no more than an hour. Even if you meet weekly, it is obviously a limited period. Furthermore, strategies discussed in therapy require time for proper implementation and practice at home or in the workplace to achieve desired results. It doesn't matter how long or frequently you meet with a therapist, if you don't apply and practice the new insights you gain, any change that results will be limited.

There may be times when clients continue to attend appointments, even though they feel that nothing is changing for them. In such circumstances it is helpful to bring up these feelings of discouragement for discussion with your therapist. Don't be afraid to ask questions or challenge your therapist. It's okay to disagree; sometimes disagreement offers the opportunity to work through conflict in a way you haven't experienced before. Perhaps together you can discover what, if anything, has been missing. Or perhaps you're not giving yourself enough credit for the work you've already put in and the progress you've already made.

MY PROBLEMS AREN'T SERIOUS ENOUGH FOR THERAPY

We all experience problems as we move through life. We all struggle with stress, fear, hope, desire for love, relationship challenges, and insecurity. Therapy can benefit anyone and everyone, not just those confronting severe and urgent problems. Fortunately, many people see therapy as an opportunity to self-actualize, gain self-knowledge, process something confusing, and determine what is most valuable to them. The bottom line is that therapy doesn't just help to pull you out of the trenches; it can also push you toward your goals.

Therapy is an open platform for exploring whatever you decide is important. I repeat, whatever YOU decide is important. People seek guidance and empowerment through therapy for a variety of reasons, and the significance of those reasons should be determined solely by the individual who is seeking such guidance.

We can reduce the stigma of therapy by recognizing and accepting a few simple statements.

1) It's okay to examine who we are.

2) It's okay to explore what is working and what isn't working in our life.

3) It's okay to want to make changes to better ourselves and get support along the way.

CHAPTER 22 ACTIVITY

In this chapter, you have learned more about therapy. Now, it's time to consider some questions that will help you in your search for a therapist, should you decide to see one. Answer the questions below and use this as a resource when exploring your options.

OUTLINE YOUR VALUES

- *Name three things that stand out to you in this chapter:*
- *What kind of location would be the best fit for you?*
- *How did you come to this conclusion?*
- *Do you have insurance and have you considered using it to cover costs? Yes / No*
- *How do you feel about having a diagnosis?*

- *Begin the online search here:*
  - » *Good Therapy* [103]
  - » *Psychology Today* [104]

  (*Good Therapy* and *Psychology Today* are online search platforms that allow you to search for therapists by location, gender, insurance panel, and many other factors.)

- *Google search*
  Possible search terms:
  - » *Therapist*
  - » *Counselor*
  - » *Psychotherapist*

» *Marriage and family therapist*
» *Substance abuse counselor*

Terms by condition/location
Example: *Depression; Counseling; Asheville, NC*

HOW TO CHOOSE A COACH, THERAPIST, OR OTHER HELPING PROFESSIONAL

This chapter will help you find the right helping professional. Many people ask me what distinguishes one kind of therapist or coach from another and how to choose the most appropriate one. Since we already know a little about the four main disciplines therapists work within and where to find a therapist, let's look at a few more criteria for choosing a therapist or other helping professional.

Just to rehash a bit, when someone is going to see a professional for some kind of personal development, the therapist or professional is going to be listed as one of the following:

- *Psychiatrist*
- *Psychologist*
- *Social worker*
- *Counselor*
- *Marriage & family therapist*
- *Life/Leadership/Executive/Career/Personal Development Coach*

Side note about mentorship: If you are looking for a mentor in business, fitness, finance, etc., the principles in this section apply. Remember, the search for a helping professional is just as much about asking yourself hard questions as it is about asking them of candidates. The clearer you are about what exactly you're looking for, the greater the likelihood that you will find the person who best suits those needs.

Even though no licensure is required to be a coach, I add it into the mix because it's a relevant and valid choice for many people. Full disclosure, I'm currently a coach and have previously been a therapist. In my role as a coach, I see just as much positive change in clients and organizations I serve as I did when practicing as a therapist. The main distinction is that in coaching and consulting work, people are typically addressing different kinds of life changes than in therapy. (More about this in the next chapter.)

In your search for a helping professional, keep in mind that one of the strongest determinants of success is the fit of the working relationship.

The question then becomes, *"How do I decide if this professional is a good fit for me?"*

As a preliminary step, you can do an online search. As mentioned in the last chapter, if you're looking for a therapist, I recommend two websites: www.psychologytoday.com and www.goodtherapy.com, which offer helpful platforms to search for therapists by specialty, location, insurance provider, etc. You can also visit individual practitioner or group practice websites to read bios and reviews. To get a more personal sense of the therapist, try a phone call. Most therapists offer free introductory calls. Finding the right coach can be a little more difficult, we'll dive into that in the next chapter.

Here are four questions to help you identify the right fit when speaking with or meeting with a prospective helping professional:

1. **How does this person communicate?**
    When you speak to a prospective helping professional, consider what kind of communicator he/she is and if his/her style is compatible with yours. Some people appreciate more direct interaction, some prefer a more inquisitive or curious nature, while others work best with someone who will listen for longer stretches, allowing more time for quiet reflection.

2. **What is their philosophy about growth and change, and does this philosophy align with mine?**
    While there are many theories about what elicits change and what leads to progress, working with someone who shares your basic philosophy is often beneficial. For example, if a helping professional believes change comes from working through someone's past issues to uncover the meaning behind behaviors (in order to better manage them in the future) and you identify with this, then perhaps this is a great fit.
    Alternatively, some people approach changes from a forward-facing perspective, according to which strengths are

identified and built upon and past stories and behaviors are examined only briefly. Perhaps his approach would serve you better.

It is up to you to determine what is congruent with your philosophy and sensibilities.

Take the time to evaluate your philosophy to be sure it is one that serves you well. For instance, if you believe that looking back at your history is irrelevant and that you've always avoided doing so, consider for a moment that your belief might just be covering up a blind spot or excusing something you fear or find painful. If such is the case, the belief may be impeding self-understanding and personal growth. (See Section 7 about beliefs, Chapter 5 about intuition, and Chapter 13 about fear.)

3. **Are the service details in line with your desires?**

   Don't neglect to consider all of the details of the prospective helping professional's services. Some of these details may include price, location, availability, experience, and practice modality. Modalities are specific ways of approaching certain client concerns. For example, certain practitioners focus on addiction with the modality I mentioned in Chapter 17, Motivational Interviewing. This modality helps clients overcome ambivalence about positive change making by exploring potential risks and rewards. I would recommend that you find a therapist, coach or helping professional who has experience with the issue that you would like to address. Reading about the person's background and asking questions for clarification will give you a better sense of compatibility.

4. **How do you feel when you are speaking with this person or in their presence?**

   When you are with this person, consider asking yourself the question, "How do I feel in this moment?" Feeling at ease, comfortable, curious, or eager to share with this person are strong indications that this could be a good fit. Of course, while first impressions can say a lot, they are not foolproof. It often requires two or three meetings or phone calls to get a clear idea of compatibility. Combining your intuition with these fundamental questions should add a sense of security to your decision-making. Bottom line: trust yourself, ask questions, and be honest.

There are many wonderful helping professionals out there with a wide variety of experiences and approaches. Remember, if you have an experience with a helping professional that is not what you are looking for, it may not indicate a poor fit. It could reflect your own discomfort in addressing an aspect of yourself that has long been neglected. Whatever it is, dialogue can be helpful. Your discomfort or a discrepancy of outlook is unlikely to be a reflection of the profession itself. Remember, *"Don't throw the baby out with the bathwater."* Seeking a professional who is a great fit should raise just as many questions about yourself as it does about the person you are looking for.

> For more information about creating changes
> or working with a helping professional,
> find some free helpful tools and strategies
> here: – www.arcintegrated.com/changes

CHAPTER 23 ACTIVITY

The questions below will help you find someone who is the best fit for you in terms of communication style, philosophy, and values. It will be valuable to track your answers in one place.

Describe three valuable exchanges you've had recently. Write down each exchange as a story, and be sure to include all the details. Specificity in your account will clarify the dynamic of the exchange.

What did you appreciate about each of the exchanges?

Describe the process by which you think positive change occurs. Use this description to help you find a helping professional that fits your needs.

Ask your prospective helping professional how they think positive change occurs. Do your descriptions match? If not, can you still work with this person? Still not sure? Share what you wrote here with your prospective helping professional, and see where the conversation goes. Take notes on this conversation and reflect on what seems promising and what might be a challenge.

What does your budget look like? Consider writing out your price range and availability prior to setting up an interview with a helping professional.

After interviewing each helping professional, write down his/her name and how you felt after speaking with them. Did you feel excited, curious, tired, inspired, or irritated? Pay attention to what your body and intuition are telling you about compatibility.

24

THE DIFFERENCE BETWEEN COACHING AND THERAPY

Choosing a coach or a therapist can be a tough decision. This chapter provides the information you need to determine which one is right for you.

Working with a therapist often concerns a pain or dysfunction that needs to be addressed. It could be related to depression, anxiety, trauma, substance abuse, or some other unresolved condition. When looking for a coach, you may be more interested in developing better business practices, advancing or changing careers, or improving your health, finances, or leadership capabilities, something new, improving something already in place, or advancing in career, health, finance, leadership, or in relationships.

As previously mentioned, the coaching is more forward-facing and goal-oriented. The International Coach Federation, a leading authority in coaching, defines the coaching process as *"a thought-provoking and creative process that inspires [clients] to maximize their personal and professional potential."* [105]

Since we've already discussed the various types of therapy, let's take a look at the different types of coaching.

Life Coaching or Personal Development Coaching – I rarely use the term, life coaching. I choose personal development coaching as an alternative term because it puts more emphasis on the client's choice. Our own development is something that we actively choose, or don't choose. Unfortunately, many people go through life without making choices that move them toward self-improvement.

Life is a given, life-development is a choice.

Personal development coaching can be related to work, relationships, finance, wellness as well as many other factors. This type of coaching may involve exploring strengths and challenges in order to build on individual passions, successes, motivations, disciplines, and experiences.

Leadership/Executive Coaching – Executive coaches often work with organizational or business leaders on improving business strategy or leadership. Alternatively, executive coaches work with clients on self-care, stress management, self-awareness, and other interpersonal dynamics that impact business. Areas that executive coaches may focus on with clients include communication, leadership, time management, team dynamics, change management, employee engagement, workplace culture, and employee/employer conflicts.

Career Coaching – Just as it sounds, with a career coach you'll explore what kind of career to start, transition from, or change. Working with a career coach may be helpful when trying to identify insight, talents, strengths, or blind spots that affect work and career options.

Similar to therapy, coaching involves setting goals and pursuing specific outcomes. Unlike therapy, however, coaching involves a forward-facing strategy and is not focused on resolving dysfunction or processing pain. While these issues may come up, the focus in coaching is primarily on action, taking steps to reach goals.

If you decide coaching is the route to take, remember that, as with therapy, there are lots of options.

Here is one way I like to visualize coaching and counseling/therapy:

COACHING VS. COUNSELING

COACHING

- Leadership
- Business Development
- Special Skills Training

- Optimizing Skills
- Strengths
- Transition

COUNSELING

- Dysfunction
- Trauma
- Substance Abuse

ARC INTEGRATED

Regardless of specialty, what qualifications should one look for in a coach? As pertinent as this question is, it's also tricky because, as with all the disciplines within the wider field of behavioral health, coaching continues to evolve. Plus, without mandatory licensure, anyone can call him or herself a coach. (As we've learned, Psychologists, Marriage and Family Therapists, Professional Counselors and Social Workers, do require licenses.)

Compared to therapy, coaching is a newer field and therefore less institutionalized. Coaching courses only provide certification, not licensure. Though not strictly necessary, you can obtain a certificate in a wide variety of coaching disciplines and areas of expertise.

Does this make coaching less credible? I don't think so. While coaching is not governed with the same level of scrutiny as are the other mental health professions, the good work performed by the highly skilled professionals in the coaching field should not be discounted.

There are many advantages to the coaching process. For instance, there are fewer restrictions pertaining to working with clients remotely. Effectively, this means that you can hire a coach from anywhere in the country just as easily as you could hire one in your own neighborhood. Many states place heavy restrictions on therapists in regard to remote work. That said, the issue of virtual client meetings within the various helping professions continues to evolve. Again, as opposed to therapy, which often addresses pain or dysfunction, the coaching process is often more forward-facing and solution-oriented, which is desirable for many clients.

Ultimately, it comes down to three questions:

- *Do you identify with this person?*

- *Do you trust this person?*
- *Do you believe you will gain valuable insight through working with this person?*

These are important questions to ask of anyone, regardless of the title they use.

In my opinion, both coaching and therapy are valuable. Your decision between them should depend on two factors: the approach you are looking for and the area in which you are seeking change.

For additional information on coaching, try the well-respected resource, The International Coaching Federation.[106] For access to more information about therapy, visit the online resources I mentioned last chapter, *Good Therapy* or *Psychology Today*.

CHAPTER 24 ACTIVITY

Beginning the Search

Honestly answering the following questions will help inform your search for a coach or therapist. Once you begin your search, use your responses as a guide to compare how the professionals explain their services. An overlap between your answers and their explanations may indicate a good fit!

1. How action-oriented do you want this process to be?

2. How much time do you want to spend processing current situations and/or past experiences?

3. Are you struggling with some kind of traumatic experience?

4. Is the change you are searching for more goal-oriented or process-oriented? If you are more interested in processing something, what form do you imagine this taking? Would it be helpful to search for the root of the problem, or would it be more pragmatic to focus primarily on current solutions?

5. Do you want to gain insight into this issue or are you just interested in changing circumstances?

When interviewing therapists or coaches during your search, you can now use your answers to these questions, as well as the previous chapter activities as material for discussion. Your answers will offer valuable clues to finding the right fit for you.

25

COACHING FOR ORGANIZATIONAL SUCCESS

N ow that you know more about the differences between coaching and therapy, let's take a closer look at the results of working with a coach. In this chapter you'll learn more about the benefits that coaching brings to individuals and organizations.

Coaches typically help individuals or organizations identify goals, set commitments, and build on strengths to institute changes that lead to growth. The demand for coaching is on the rise. As of 2019 numerous universities offer coaching certificate programs. The most prestigious include Northwestern, Columbia, UC Berkeley, George Washington, and Harvard. In addition to these highly reputable universities, there are also hundreds of other coaching programs that are less selective. For a comprehensive list, consult the International Coach Federation (ICF), the major accrediting institute for all coach-training programs.[107]

In the last chapter, we reviewed various coaching specializations. Despite the various types, there is also much convergence. For instance, personal development coaching overlaps with all other types of coaching since exploring our beliefs, behaviors, aspirations, and expectations pertain to our career, relationships, and just about any change we are seeking.

In the coming pages, we'll explore what it means to be coached and, in particular, how a coach is relevant to business and organizational success.

A couple things to remember from the last chapter:

- *The field of coaching encompasses a variety of specializations including: executive coaching, life/personal development coaching, leadership coaching, and career coaching.*
- *Coaching usually does not have an emphasis on processing a particular pain or dysfunction. There is more emphasis on goal setting and personal optimization.*

I think it may be helpful at this point to describe the actual process of working with a coach. In many ways, it's similar to working with a therapist. Typically, coaching begins with some paperwork and discussion about goals and desired changes to be made within a certain time frame (six months, for example). Like therapists, coaches often use assessments, but they do so for different purposes. Coaching assessments help clients build insight into various workplace or professional attributes such as leadership, communication, motivation, and emotional intelligence. Coaches work with clients in 60-90 minute sessions in person or remotely. The frequency (weekly, monthly, etc.) depends on the coach's recommendation and the client's resources.

The International Coaching Federation (ICF), the leading professional organization for coaches, has about 25,000 members. Also, according to the ICF, the number of coaches in America has tripled in the last 10 years.[108] As coaching evolves and becomes even more popular, this number is expected to grow at its current steep rate. The two most reported reasons people seek coaching are work-life balance and personal growth. According to The Center for Creative Leadership, coaching can also improve self-awareness, improve understanding of others, enhance the ability to communicate as well as enhance the ability to coach others.[109]

Coaching is also popular and effective for organizations as a whole. According to a study by The Miles Group and Stanford University, nearly one-third of all executives work with coaches, while nearly 100 percent report desiring a coach.[110] The study also found that 43 percent of executives reported conflict management as their top priority in seeking a coach. Turning to coaching to develop leadership and communication skills also ranks highly.

While making improvements in conflict management, leadership, and communication skills is important, there are underlying principles that must be developed first as a foundation for those goals. Principles such as compassion, empathy, and self-awareness have been proven to be valuable assets to executives.[111]

Coaching can offer great insight into the needs and concerns across an organizational hierarchy. For example, research by the Kellogg School of Management at Northwestern University suggests that as one's professional power increases, one's empathy decreases.[112] In this respect, coaching on self-awareness and empathy can play a corrective role in effecting personal and organizational success. As one assumes a greater leadership role, one bears greater responsibilities. Foremost among these is connecting with others, an essential quality of effective leaders.

Coaching is not just about improving the organizational bottom line, although this is often the result. Coaching can also impact professionals at the personal level. According to a survey by the *Harvard Business Review*, while only 3 percent of coaches were intentionally hired to help address a personal issue, 76 percent report having assisted executives with personal issues.[113] These figures suggest that while personal issues are a key focus in executive coaching scenarios, there is still a general misunderstanding about how entangled business and personal development truly are. Clearly, there is a demand for coaching, especially when people are honest with themselves. The survey also revealed that those who had a desire to learn and grow and were willing to address personal issues experienced the greatest success with executive coaching.

So, you may be asking, what is the true financial return on investment (ROI) when working with a coach? According to a study by Manchester Consulting Group, which looked at Fortune 100 executives who had received coaching, there was an ROI of six times the cost of the coaching program.[114] Coaching resulted in improvements in relationships, teamwork, and job satisfaction across organizations.

But what kind of organizations are implementing coaching? You may think this is only for Fortune 500 companies. Not so. In addition to working with global corporations, I have consulted with a wide range of small organizations, including individual startups with minimal staff and family-owned businesses. In addition, I have worked with clients in a variety of industries from global manufacturing to higher education to landscaping. The value of coaching does not depend on what field you are in or the size of the company you work for. You don't need to be

Google to invest in your workplace culture, prioritize employee satisfaction, or set up opportunities for trust, transparency, positive communication, and inspiration-based leadership. You also certainly don't need to be a corporate CEO to invest in your own continued development, which will absolutely impact your business's bottom line.

Development is vital in any industry. For instance, I once worked with a company in the landscaping industry that was invested in its workplace culture, employee development, and personal and professional development. I worked with the leadership team as well as employees. The company leaders are of particular relevance to this book. They were able to see how communication, leadership, and emotional intelligence impacted the bottom line. Moreover, they came to understand how their communication style, management of stress, and general disposition as leaders also played a role in their personal lives. Having discovered how the parts of their development were connected, they were able to take aspects of our work and apply it to their lives outside of work. Through our hard work, we uncovered valuable insights into how they managed stress at home and how they engaged with their families.

My hope for all my clients is that they can connect professional and personal development to ensure the success of both.

Your success depends on your personal level of commitment and readiness for change. If you are ready to take a look inward to uncover your barriers to success, then coaching is a great choice.

CHAPTER 25 ACTIVITY

Explore the following questions and consider how each leads to an action step. This activity will help you decide if coaching is right for you and, if so, will help you determine what kind of coach would be the most fitting, given your current needs.

Understanding what you want and how to get it is important. The next step is to ask for it.

Does your organization have an internal coaching program? If not, consider presenting some of the data from this chapter to a leader in the organization to start the conversation about implementing such a program. Perhaps it would also be useful to inquire about your organization sponsoring your coaching as a component to your professional development. Yes, organizations do this. We see it all the time.

What would be the added value to your organization if you pursued coaching?

More specifically, if you were to work with a coach, what types of outcomes would most benefit your organization (leadership, emotional intelligence, productivity, delegation, etc.)?

What would be the value of pursuing coaching independent of your organization?

Based on what you have learned about the benefits of coaching so far, what value do you think a coach would add to your pursuit of personal or professional goals?

Journal about how you would create connections between personal development and your ability to succeed in your career.

Refer to your responses as you consider which coach is the right fit. Also, consider sharing your written responses with coaching candidates. Your responses will offer the coach a window into who you are. They may also serve as a springboard to a robust conversation that will help you determine goodness of fit.

Finally, write down at least one detailed action you will commit to in the next two weeks.

AFTERWORD

I t was an honor to write this book and a pleasure to revisit so many stories, those of others and my own. Some uplifting, some painful and all totally valuable. For this reflection process and to everyone who inspired the content of these stories, I remain grateful.

Throughout the writing of this book, I kept thinking about the consistency of change. It's one of the few absolutes. I have faith that the concepts in this book will remain helpful in this changing world. At the same time, I'm also confident that what we understand about how we make change in our lives, will always be evolving. This evolution need not inspire fear of the unknown. Instead, it can feed our curiosity and spark excitement.

For now, don't underestimate the serious potential of integrating the various parts of your lived experience. If we are being held back from what we want to change in our life, there is a reason, and oftentimes, it is in our control. Even if the only thing we can control is our perspective, as we've seen, this shift can change our very reality.

After doing all the research, reassessing client stories, and examining the tools available to us, I am more convinced than ever that connecting the various parts of our lived experience leads to positive change.

As we set out to create the lives we want, let's continue to focus on this connectivity.

THANK YOU SO MUCH!

I appreciate you reading my book "CHANGES – The Busy Professional's Guide to Reducing Stress, Accomplishing Goals, and Mastering Adaptability."

If you found value here, please leave a helpful REVIEW with your favorite book distributor or on Amazon.

Thanks in advance for all your feedback. Wishing you success in all your pursuits of positive change!

—Michael

ACKNOWLEDGMENTS

To say that a book has a single author seems kind of silly at this point. I wonder how many authors out there feel that they alone are to take credit/blame for their work. This book is the culmination of four years of work. What launched as a writing project underwent quite a transformation before landing. It's gone through not only many editing rounds, but also major concept changes. I give this short bit of background because I want to give credit where it's due. Without the support of so many people, I'm not sure there would be any fruit to bear here.

Since this book is somewhat of a chronicle of my own personal and professional experiences and observations, it seems fitting that I acknowledge the clients, friends, family, teachers, lovers, supporters, (even naysayers!) who have played a significant role in informing my philosophy. I remain grateful.

I would like to take the opportunity to acknowledge those whose general influence and specific input were absolutely critical to the development of this book. To my parents, Lynn Diettrich and David Chastain, for their unconditional love, support, and belief in me. To my extended family and friends for their love, support, and entertainment. You know who you are.

Robin Adams your love, support, and belief in this (very time-consuming) project have kept me going. Much love to you, my dear. Thank you for being my biggest fan.

ACKNOWLEDGMENTS

All the organizations, individuals, families, couples, leaders, and teams I have worked with over the years, thank you for your willingness to share your stories.

Sam Uhl at The Cheerful Word publishing house, thank you for your support and encouragement during the beginning of this book and for your encouragement to re-frame it.

Dr. Keith Davis, Dr. Sally Atkins, Dr. Jack Mulgrew, and all the professors at Appalachian State University, thank you for kindling my passion for understanding how people create change in their lives.

Grandmaster Rick Ward, you remain a significant influence in my pursuits of the martial arts as well as on my philosophy of life. Thank you, Sifu. Thanks to all my teachers, training partners, and students of Blue Ridge Kung Fu Arnis Academy as well. I continue to be amazed by the depth of wisdom to be found in the martial arts.

Matt Moseley, thank you for your coaching, late night discussions, writing tips, friendship, and constant encouragement. Keep howling at the moon, sir!

Ryan Carrasco, thank you for your excellent questions, conceptual challenges, and editing prowess. Without you, sir, this book would not have developed as it did. So much gratitude for you!

Chandler Bolt, Sean Sumner, Lise Cartwright and all of the folks at The Self Publishing School, thank you for continuing to educate me on all things Indie and Traditional Publishing. Many thanks for your guidance!

Catherine, the crew at Bright Planning, and the launch team, thank you for your enthusiasm, patience, and rallying when it really mattered.

Christos Angelidakis, thank you for your sharing your design prowess and for showing much patience. I appreciate you hanging in there with me.

Thank you to Rachel McCracken and the folks at Chasing Kites as well as Matías Baldanza for the design and book formatting expertise!

Finally, if you are reading this, thank you for putting your trust in me. I hope the materials within challenge you to think, act, consider, respond, and explore in new, more dynamic ways. Best wishes to you on your journey!

NOTES

INTRODUCTION

1. Biopsychosocial model.
   http://sk.sagepub.com/reference/the-sage-encyclopedia-of-theory-in-counseling-and -psychotherapy/i2350.xml

CHAPTER 1

2. Man's Search for Meaning.
   https://www.amazon.com/Mans-Search-Meaning-Viktor-Frankl/dp/080701429X/ref=sr_1_1?ie=UTF8&qid=1525975696&sr=8-1&keywords=mans+search+for+meaning

3. Victor Frankl, Victor.'s Logotherapy.
   https://www.goodtherapy.org/learn--about--therapy/types/logotherapy

CHAPTER 2

4. *Journal of College and Character*, Strengths and why they are important.
   https://www.tandfonline.com/doi/pdf/10.2202/1940-1639.1042

CHAPTER 4

5. *The Industrial Psychiatry Journal* emotional intelligence definition: *"The ability to monitor one's own and other people's emotions, to discriminate between different emotions and label them appropriately, and to use emotional information to guide thinking and behavior."*

6. Daniel Goleman's definition of emotional intelligence.
   http://www.danielgoleman.info/
   daniel-goleman-how-emotionally-intelligent-are-you/

7. Talent Smart Research, business case for EQ.
   http://www.talentsmart.com/about/emotional-intelligence.php

8. Situational Leadership.
   https://en.wikipedia.org/wiki/Situational_leadership_theory

9. The Graduate School of Applied and Professional Psychology at
   Rutgers University,The business case for emotional intelligence
   http://www.eiconsortium.org/reports/business_case_for_ei.html

10. *The Journal of Marketing*, Stress management and retail store profit
    https://www.jstor.org/
    stable/1252175?seq=1#page_scan_tab_contents

11. Organizational Dynamics, Increase in manufacturing production
    https://www.sciencedirect.com/science/article/
    pii/0090261681900267

12. Center for Creative Leadership Study, consequences of deficits in
    emotional intelligence.
    https://www.ccl.org/wp-content/uploads/2015/04/
    BenchmarksSourcebook.pdf

13. *Journal of Personality, Emotional intelligence and Health*, Higher EQ
    and better health
    http://www.sciencedirect.com/science/article/pii/
    S0191886906003539

CHAPTER 5

14. *Oxford Dictionary*, Definition for Intuition
    https://en.oxforddictionaries.com/definition/intuition

15. *Science*, Deciding advantageously before knowing the advantageous strategy

16. On making the right choice: the deliberation-without-attention effect.

17. Tapping into unconscious intuition

CHAPTER 6

18. The Global Rich List.
    http://www.globalrichlist.com/

19. Top 1% in the U.S.

20. Robert Emmons, Benefits of Gratitude.
    http://greatergood.berkeley.edu/article/item/
    why_gratitude_is_good

21. *Journal of the Society for Psychotherapy Research*, Gratitude writing
    and mental health
    https://www.tandfonline.com/doi/abs/10.1080/10503307.2016.
    1169332?scroll=top&needAccess=true&journalCode=tpsr20

22. Gottman research on gratitude and relationships
    https://www.gottman.com/blog/
    the-magic-relationship-ratio-according-science/

CHAPTER 7

23. Will Bowen complaint free world
    https://www.willbowen.com/complaintfree/

24. Will Bowen, complaint free world, complaining experiment timing
    https://www.willbowen.com/complaintfree/

CHAPTER 8

25. *Business Insider*, Richard Branson always carries a notebook
    https://www.businessinsider.com/
    richard-branson-productivity-hack-2014-9

26. Brene Brown, shame and guilt
https://www.ted.com/talks/
brene_brown_listening_to_shame#t-412159

CHAPTER 9

27. *Comidor*, Boosting Personal Productivity in Real Life
https://www.comidor.com/cms.php/
en/blog/enterprise-collaboration/
boosting-personal-productivity-in-real-life

28. *Fast Company*, Traits of successful people.
https://www.fastcompany.com/3038843/
the-common-traits-of-the-most-successful-people

29. *Forbes*, Sitting is the new smoking.
http://www.forbes.com/sites/davidsturt/2015/01/13/
is-sitting-the-new-smoking/#25fc9d67239a

CHAPTER 10

30. *The Guardian*, Body mind connection
https://www.theguardian.com/lifeandstyle/2015/jan/04/
depression-allergic-reaction-inflammation-immune-
system?CMP=share_btn_fb

31. National Institute of Mental Health, Mental health and Chronic
Illness
https://www.nimh.nih.gov/health/publications/chronic-illness-
mental-health-2015/index.shtml

32. Healthline, *"The Effects of Depression in Your Body"*
http://www.healthline.com/health/depression/effects-on-body

33. Depression caused by chronic illness
http://www.medicinenet.com/script/main/art.
asp?articlekey=55170

34. *Journal of Palliative Medicine*, Mind body approach in treatment
http://online.liebertpub.com/doi/abs/10.1089/jpm.2009.0143

35. *Canadian Journal of Counselling and Psychotherapy*, Yoga and therapy
    http://files.eric.ed.gov/fulltext/EJ930795.pdf

36. Stress and Health, Multimodal stress reduction program for teachers.

37. The Model Health Show.
    http://theshawnstevensonmodel.com/

38. The Tim Ferriss Show.
    https://tim.blog/podcast/

39. The Aubrey Marcus Podcast.
    https://www.aubreymarcus.com/blogs/aubrey-marcus/tagged/aubrey-marcus-podcast

CHAPTER 11

40. Psych Central, *"What is self-care"* by Dr. Agnes Wainman
    https://psychcentral.com/blog/what-self-care-is-and-what-it-isnt-2/

41. Self-care improves healing experience & organizational health
    http://www.news-medical.net/news/20100813/Research-reveals-self-care-improves-healing-experience.aspx

42. *Own the Day, Own Your Life.* Aubrey Marcus.
    https://www.amazon.com/Own-Day-Your-Life-Optimized/dp/0062684078

43. Science behind the value of sex.
    https://www.webmd.com/sex-relationships/guide/sex-and-health#1

CHAPTER 12

44. What is qigong.
    https://www.nqa.org/what-is-qigong-

45. UCLA study of meditation impact on aging
    https://www.frontiersin.org/articles/10.3389/fpsyg.2014.01551/full

46. Mayo Clinic, Meditation and stress reduction.
    http://www.mayoclinic.org/tests-procedures/meditation/in-depth/meditation/art-20045858

47. Johns Hopkins Study, Meditation programs for psychological stress and well being.
    http://jamanetwork.com/journals/jamainternalmedicine/fullarticle/1809754

48. Meditation and smoking cessation.

49. *Harvard Health Publishing*, Meditation and absenteeism.
    https://www.health.harvard.edu/newsletter_article/mental-health-problems-in-the-workplace

50. *World Health Organization*, Depression as leading cause of disability Meditation and disability.
    https://www.who.int/news-room/fact-sheets/detail/depression

51. Aetna's mindfulness program, meditation, healthcare, and productivity.
    https://news.aetna.com/2014/09/journey-personal-organizational-wellness/

52. *TIME* article, Meditation and mindfulness in the workplace.
    http://time.com/4624276/yoga-workplace-mindfulness/

53. MUSE, the brain sensing headband.
    http://www.choosemuse.com/how-does-muse-work/

CHAPTER 14

54. The Whole 30®.
    https://whole30.com/whole30-program-rules/

55. The Positive Psychology Center at the University of Pennsylvania, self discipline and IQ.
    http://pss.sagepub.com/content/16/12/939.short

56. *The Journal of Applied Developmental Psychology*, Discipline and martial arts.
http://www.sciencedirect.com/science/article/pii/S0193397304000309

57. Washington University's Department of Psychology, Discipline in older adults.
http://psychsocgerontology.oxfordjournals.org/content/60/3/P153.short

58. *The Journal of Depression and Anxiety*, Discipline and depression.
http://onlinelibrary.wiley.com/doi/10.1002/da.20026/abstract

CHAPTER 15

59. Gallup research, ROI for building strengths.
http://www.gallup.com/businessjournal/167462/employees-strengths-company-stronger.aspx

CHAPTER 16

60. Inspire Me Today, 500 words of wisdom.
http://inspiremetoday.com/brilliance/mindful-courageous-adventurous/

61. Gallup, Employee engagement and turnover.
http://www.gallup.com/businessjournal/163130/employee-engagement-drives-growth.aspx

62. Gallup, Five tips to improve employee engagement.
https://www.gallup.com/workplace/231581/five-ways-improve-employee-engagement.aspx

63. *Harvard Health Publishing*, Appreciation and workplace environment.
https://www.health.harvard.edu/newsletter_article/in-praise-of-gratitude

64. IBM study on Inspiring leadership.
    http://www-935.ibm.com/services/multimedia/anz_ceo_
    study_2012.pdf

65. *Forbes*, Carmine Gallo on 7 ways to be inspiring as a leader.
    https://www.forbes.com/sites/carminegallo/2011/07/06/
    the-7-secrets-of-inspiring-leaders/#649cda0d1433

66. Value alignment and engagement.
    https://www.bizjournals.com/bizjournals/how-to/growth-
    strategies/2014/06/how-to-get-employees-to-align-with-
    company-mission.html

67. Engagement and operating income, Towers Watson.
    https://www.towerswatson.com/DownloadMedia.
    aspx?media=%7BE87F6E65-99E6-413B-8068-09B6821FA7BF%7D

68. The Social Workplace, List of studies on employee engagement.
    http://www.thesocialworkplace.com/2011/08/social-knows-
    employee-engagement-statistics-august-2011-edition/

CHAPTER 17

69. *The Journal of Occupational Health*, Listening skills at work.
    https://www.jstage.jst.go.jp/article/joh/49/2/49_2_81/_article

70. Small Group Research, Leadership and listening.
    http://journals.sagepub.com/doi/
    abs/10.1177/1046496498294003

71. Motivational Interviewing.
    https://www.ihs.gov/california/tasks/sites/default/assets/File/
    BP2015-4_TeachingSBIRTFacultyGuideSession3Part2.pdf

CHAPTER 18

72. *Livestrong*, 7 Ways to set Clear Boundaries with People in
    Your Life.
    https://www.livestrong.com/
    slideshow/1011354-people-need-set-boundaries/

73. *The Academy of Management Journal,* Between You and Me: Setting Work-Nonwork Boundaries in the Context of Workplace Relationships.
http://amj.aom.org/content/56/6/1802.short

74. The University of California, San Francisco, Healthy workplace boundaries.
https://hr.ucsf.edu/hr.php?A=1069&AT=cm&org=c&sref=5

CHAPTER 19

75. Biological impacts of meditation.
https://books.google.com/books?hl=en&lr=&id=aFe1DA
AAQBAJ&oi=fnd&pg=PA175&dq=biological+impact+of
+meditation&ots=yh0W9DWgYa&sig=WoSsB3oUs4XPx
PH-VwpkxBEgya0#v=onepage&q&f=false

CHAPTER 20

76. *The Journal of Behavioral Medicine,* Spirituality relates to emotional well being and quality of life.
https://www.ncbi.nlm.nih.gov/pubmed/15194519

77. *The Journal of Health Psychology,* Religious coping methods impact health.
http://journals.sagepub.com/doi/
abs/10.1177/1359105304045366

78. Meta-analysis of religious coping related to stress.

79. *The International Journal of Indian Psychology*, spirituality and inspired leadership.
https://books.google.com/books?id=245cDAAAQBAJ&pg=PA142
&lpg=PA142&dq=The+International+Journal+of+Indian+Psycholo
gy,+spirituality+in+the+workplace+is+related+to+inspired+leader
ship&source=bl&ots=GmmnXgcvGE&sig=8UETjN2d_qvl3VmA7
T2tuNGvKsg&hl=en&sa=X&ved=0ahUKEwi4k_au8dLWAhUszoM
KHcOpDlcQ6AEIJjAA#v=onepage&q=The%20International%20
Journal%20of%20Indian%20Psychology%2C%20spirituality%20

in%20the%20workplace%20is%20related%20to%20inspired%20
leadership&f=false

80. *Personality and Individual Differences*, Spirituality and workplace conflict.
http://www.sciencedirect.com/science/article/pii/
S0191886912002991

CHAPTER 21

81. Current Biology, Mental imagery changes perception.
https://www.ncbi.nlm.nih.gov/pubmed/23810539?otool=karolib
&tool=karolinska

82. Belief, self-efficacy and health.

83. *The Journal of Research in Personality*, Openness to experience and
bio changes.
http://www.sciencedirect.com/science/article/pii/
S0092656617300338?dgcid=raven_sd_via_email

84. Cell mediated Immunity.
https://www.ncbi.nlm.nih.gov/pmc/articles/PMC3933956/

85. Placebo effect and pain, anxiety, Parkinson's disease, and some
surgical procedures.
http://www.sciencedirect.com/science/article/pii/
S030645221500740X

CHANGES IN MOTION

86. Jack Canfield's how to create a vision board.
http://jackcanfield.com/blog/
how-to-create-an-empowering-vision-book/

87. Strategies for achieving goals.
http://www.dominican.edu/dominicannews/
study-highlights-strategies-for-achieving-goals

CHAPTER 22

88. Psychotherapy is a 15-billion-dollar industry.
http://www.ibisworld.com/industry/default.aspx?indid=1561

89. Definition of Psychology from American
Psychological Association.

90. Definition of Social Work from National Association of
Social Work.
https://www.socialworkers.org/Practice

91. Definition of Marriage and Family Therapy from the American
Association for Marriage and Family Therapy.
https://www.aamft.org/About_AAMFT/
About_Marriage_and_Family_Therapists.
aspx?hkey=1c77b71c-0331-417b-b59b-34358d32b909

92. Definition of Counseling from the American Counseling
Association .
https://www.counseling.org/about-us/about-
aca/20-20-a-vision-for-the-future-of-counseling/
consensus-definition-of-counseling

93. Definition Psychiatry from American Psychiatric Association.
https://www.psychiatry.org/patients-families/what-is-psychiatry

94. Definition of Advanced Practice Psychiatric Mental Health
Nurses, The American Psychiatric Nurses Association.
https://www.apna.org/i4a/pages/index.cfm?pageID=3857

95. Increased MH services in hospitals.
http://www.hhnmag.com/articles/3476-four-ways-hospitals-are-
improving-behavioral-health-care

96. Integrated healthcare model.
http://ct.counseling.org/tag/integrated-care/

97. *Law and Human Behavior Journal*, MH intervention reduces recidivism.
https://www.ncbi.nlm.nih.gov/pmc/articles/PMC3266968/

98. *The American Journal of Public Health*, Mental health in prisons.

99. World Psychiatry, Change in mental health treatment in prisons.
https://www.ncbi.nlm.nih.gov/pmc/articles/PMC5269683/

100. Complexities of having a MH diagnosis.
https://www.ncbi.nlm.nih.gov/pubmed/27796258

101. Reducing the stigma of MH.
https://www.ncbi.nlm.nih.gov/pmc/articles/PMC3839682/

102. Research around the therapeutic alliance.
https://www.ncbi.nlm.nih.gov/pmc/articles/PMC3198542/

103. Good Therapy.
https://www.goodtherapy.org/

104. Psychology Today.
https://www.psychologytoday.com/

CHAPTER 24

105. International Coach Federation.
https://coachfederation.org/

106. International Coach Federation.
https://coachfederation.org/

CHAPTER 25

107. International Coach Federation, Accredited programs.
https://coachfederation.org/icf-credential/
find-a-training-program

108. Coaching on the rise in the last 10 years.
https://www.td.org/Publications/
Magazines/TD/TD-Archive/2012/09/
Intelligence-Coaching-Profession-Shows-Growth

109. Center for Creative Leadership study.
https://www.ccl.org/multimedia/podcast/coaching-for-results/

110. Nearly one-third of all executives receive coaching, while 100% report to want it.
http://www.gsb.stanford.edu/faculty-research/publications/2013-executive-coaching-survey

111. Forbes article about a case for empathy.
https://www.forbes.com/sites/forbescoachescouncil/2018/01/25/the-case-for-empathy-and-why-leaders-should-care/#3d91ab635442

112. Kellogg School of Management, Northwestern University, as power increases, one's ability to understand how others feel and think, decreases.
http://pss.sagepub.com/content/17/12/1068.abstract

113. *Harvard Business Review*, while only 3% of coaches were hired to help address a personal issue, 76% report to have assisted executives with personal issues.
https://hbr.org/2009/01/what-can-coaches-do-for-you

114. Coaching ROI Manchester consulting group study.
http://www.coachfederation.org/files/includes/docs/049ManchesterReviewMaximizingImpactofExecCoaching2.pdf?_ga=1.47916964.2003566038.1429743308

ABOUT THE AUTHOR

Michael is an author, speaker, professional coach, facilitator, and founder and CEO of Arc Integrated, an organizational consulting and professional coaching practice. Through a focus on emotional intelligence, leadership, and communication, Arc Integrated empowers leaders, teams and organizations to achieve optimum performance through a process of assessment, training, and coaching. You can reach Michael and his team at Arc Integrated at www.arcintegrated.com.